150 TECHNIQUES IN ART

150 TECHNIQUES IN ART

Hans Meyers

B. T. BATSFORD LTD LONDON

First English Language Edition 1963

PRINTED AND BOUND IN DENMARK
BY F. E. BORDING LTD, COPENHAGEN AND LONDON
FOR THE PUBLISHERS
B. T. BATSFORD LTD
4, FITZHARDINGE STREET, LONDON, W. 1

Preface

This volume aims to be a practical guide, in the manner of a reference work, to a large number of simple techniques. Most of these can be adapted to almost any age group.

The arrangement in the text does not mean that each succeeding exercise represents a more advanced stage. A beginning can be made with any technique, depending purely on the needs of the class or the individual pupil. In each case, first the necessary materials are enumerated, and then the technique itself is explained.

Contents

List of Illustrations

Direct Painting with Colored Blackboard Chalks (B 1 and O 1), 'Large Fruit Bowl', by a group of eleven-year-old children. Length 40 inches

A DRAWING TECHNIQUES

Pencil Drawing — A1

Medium hard pencil, such as HB (degrees of hardness range from 7B, very soft, to 9H, very hard). Any kind of paper (it is interesting to experiment in smooth and rough, thick and thin, absorbent and almost non-absorbent varieties).

Work should be based on the free, spontaneous drawing of children, which, if properly encouraged, will quite naturally lead to the descriptive and narrative drawing of the older age groups. Those inclined to draw in small timid strokes should find the courage to bold and continuous lines. The pencil should not be pressed against the paper too hard, or the result will be a greasy shine; and thin lines produce a rather insipid effect. Lines should never be retraced to make them more distinct, if the drawing is not to lose all its vigor and spontaneity. Erasers should be used most sparingly. Pen drawing will be of help as a preliminary exercise (A4). The technique described under A4 can also be adapted to pencil drawing for the older age groups.

Chalk and Crayon Drawing — A2

Pastels, black and white chalk, wax crayons, etc., paper as under A1, fixative.

Soft and medium-hard chalks are preferable. They should be used in pieces of about 1½ inches, both flat and pointed (pointed to draw lines and flat to cover whole areas). Depending on the pressure, one will obtain stronger or weaker tones. The easy handling of the medium (*Plate 25*) must not tempt to cheap effects. Except for wax crayons, these media will smudge easily. They should therefore be fixed with a spray. (For drawing and painting with blackboard chalks see B1.)

A3 Charcoal Drawing

Charcoal, a large sheet of a fairly rough paper—possibly brown paper, wallpaper remains, or newspaper; fixative (optional).

Technique as under A2. Charcoal produces lines of a mat silvery gray, and not, as one might expect, black. Here, too, the easily managed technique can tempt to quick and superficial effects. Therefore, use the material either in a 'free' technique on scrap paper (see also C2) or in work demanding considerable discipline. Charcoal is also suitable for preliminary sketches for work to be carried out in other materials (see B3d, B12 and 13; also *Plate 2a*). Since it smudges easily, the use of a fixative is advisable (see A2).

A4 Pen Drawing

Writing or drawing pens, also homemade reed pens, goose quills, etc.; black, sepia, and colored drawing ink, a fairly smooth and non-absorbent paper (see A1).

Pen and ink can be used for drawing as soon as children begin to write with them. The children should always draw and not merely trace work done first in pencil. Pencil sketches, if used at all, should never be more than a vague suggestion, to be followed only very generally (*Plate 2b*), or the spontaneous character of the work will be lost.

On a more advanced level, special exercises to increase the range of the 'palette' of the pen are possible. These exercises need not be dull and academic. The children can collect all kinds of small objects—bark, moss, leather and cloth fragments, etc.—with interesting surface texture, which can give rise to innumerable experiments with pen and paper, and may inspire a whole range of new subjects ('Scarecrow,' 'Ragpicker,' 'Old Trees,' etc).

Brush Drawing

A5

Sable brush (watercolor and poster color brush), bristle brush, and flat brushes with long, medium-long, and short bristles; inks as under A3, watercolors, paper as under A1. It is interesting to experiment with contrasts between absorbent and non-absorbent paper.

Brush drawing has an immediate appeal to children. Even the small child 'paints' the outlines, thus giving painting the character of drawing (see B3, Outline Painting).

As in pen drawing, the work should be spontaneous (see A3). Only one color should be used at first. There are several techniques, depending on the type of brush or the paper (heavily glued paper will be more suitable for firm, absorbent paper for soft, outlines), quite apart from modes of drawing. Emphasis can be on outline or on detail, producing the effect of a woodcut (*Plate 4b*). A general chiaroscuro will tire the eyes and is to be avoided. Contrasts between figures and background—light against dark, or vice versa—should be fairly marked. It is quite permissible to introduce a second color, either for lines or a wash.

A word about the care of brushes. Brushes should never be bought unless the wet hairs will form a sharp point or edge and show great resilience, returning at once to their original shape and constituting a compact mass suitable for the absorption of as much liquid as possible. They should always be cleaned immediately after use and must never be allowed to stand in the jar, not even during painting.

Wet Drawing

A6

Pens or brushes as under A4 and A5, drawing ink as under A3. The paper should not be too absorbent (see A1).

Wet drawing with soluble colors (ink, drawing ink, watercolors) allows the most varied and delightful effects. The possibilities of the blurred outline of drawing ink, applied with brush or pencil to a wet or damp ground, are best discovered in free experiment. The beginner should therefore be allowed to treat the technique simply as a way of gaining a less rigid approach to drawing. Later, he will have to learn to control 'accidental' effects. The degree of dampness, the re-damping of dried patches, and the redirection of the flow of the ink are of great importance, as is the quality of the paper. As elsewhere, a certain discipline is essential, if one is to avoid all-too-easily obtained effects or lack of form.

B PAINTING TECHNIQUES

Painting with Colored Blackboard Chalks B1

Blackboard chalks, blackboard or wrapping paper, also wall-paper, etc. An insect spray gun and fixative will prove useful in the case of paper or cardboard.

Painting and drawing on the blackboard or on large sheets of paper would appear to be the most obvious artistic activity for all age groups. Unfortunately, this is not always fully understood. The advantages of this technique can hardly be exaggerated. No drawing lesson ought to pass in the lower grades without as many children as possible having used their blackboards. A large blackboard should be constantly available to the children. The large format, the healthy movement involved, and the possibility of easy correction contribute greatly to the vigor and spontaneity of this form of art. The technique is easily learned. When the colors are used over whole areas, the ground —which ought to be kept free of color in most cases, leaving figures and objects to stand out all the more—should not be allowed to shine through. On rough papers, blackboard chalks will produce the same effect as pastels (*Plate 1*).

Painting with Pastels and Crayons B2

Pastels, medium and soft wax or oil crayons, etc., paper as under A 1, as well as almost any fairly strong variety.

Children usually take to pastels very quickly. The question inevitably arises whether the technique might not prove an obstacle to more advanced forms of art. Pastels smear easily, and without taking some care, work and hands are soon dirty. Oil crayons are generally preferable, though colored pencils are not ideal for smaller children because they involve constant sharpening and therefore interruption. The child will usually draw first and then fill in the color by shading (*Plate 9b*). Both methods lend themselves to further development by emphasis on clear articulation of every stroke, by keeping the shading within the chosen outline, and by shading very closely so that the paper is almost completely covered. If, in addition, the colors are not applied too feebly, the picture will have an intense luminosity that can stand comparison with any other painting technique (*Plate 25*). A more 'painterly' handling of the medium, by not confining areas to one particular color, is more suitable for later age groups when a preliminary pencil sketch, or even a very faint drawing, would not necessarily be out of place, though 'direct' painting should never be abandoned. But everything must depend on the way the pupil comes to terms with his medium.

B3 Painting with Poster Colors

Paint boxes with six or twelve comparatively large trays of poster color, brushes as under A5, paper as under A1, using a large format.

a. Direct Painting

Painting without a drawing in pencil or any other medium encourages free expression and the unlimited exploitation of the potentialities of color (*Plate 21a*). After the first stage, when the emphasis will have been on the general effect of the picture, one can go into greater detail by adding further touches with the brush, by partly overpainting, etc. (*Plate 24b*). Here, the great advantage of poster colors is obvious, particularly in the work of children and adolescents. Unlike in the case of watercolors, whole areas can be painted over, and a picture can thus be worked almost indefinitely.

b. Outline Painting and Filling-in

This technique, one of the oldest in the arts of mankind, has almost infinite possibilities. From it can develop painting in tempera, oils, etc. The first step, at least for the younger age groups, is a clear and distinct brush drawing (no 'impressionist' vagueness), the areas then being filled in. The most suitable subjects are those involving large figures ('My Friend and I,' (*Plate 3b*), 'Madonna and Child,' etc). Large sheets of paper should be used. While more than one color is rarely used (usually, though not always, dark) in the outline drawing, one need in no way limit oneself in the second stage, always bearing in mind the need for color harmony. Nor must the color of the ground be too strong, or it will tend to swamp the figures (*Plate 6*).

c. Colored Pencil Drawing

Where it is a matter of objective representation rather than free expression (in contrast to B3a), begin with a pencil drawing, based on careful previous observation. Up to the fourteenth year, drawing should normally be made from memory and not from nature. This technique can also be applied to purely imaginative subjects ('The Ghost Ship,' 'Creation of the Animals,') if some degree of 'precision' is required. It should be realized that it will be very much easier to keep within the outlines if the brush is held vertically, working outwards from the middle of the area to be colored. Though fairly thick and opaque, the color should always be applied liquid. In the course of the work, the penciled outline will assume less and less importance. Eventually, it may even disappear. Erasures should not be necessary, since the drawing will in any case have been very delicate and purely a guide (*Plate 3a*). Any retracing with thick strokes would be little more than an act of barbarism. Details can also be worked out as under B3a.

d. Colored Charcoal Drawing

The method described under B3c is also suitable for charcoal drawings. The charcoal should not be applied too thickly, and only in line (no shading, etc). The outline can be left standing or painted over (possibly fixed afterwards, see A2). For further detail, see B3a and c. This technique, which again requires large areas and is therefore best suited to large figure subjects, can lead directly to tempera and fresco painting (see B12).

B4 Gouache

Poster or designer colors (see B3) and a tube of white (usually included in paint boxes), brush (see B3), paper (see A1).

In gouache, colors are made opaque by mixing with white. It is, of course, possible to mix all colors. Mixing colors should begin fairly soon, certainly not later than at the age of ten or eleven. The children's interest can be aroused in many ways. Boys usually enjoy an exercise in which each color is mixed in turn with all the others, thus establishing a 'scientific' scale. No white should at first be used in this connection. But a start can also be made with Ostwald's color circle. The colors are arranged in the form of a wheel, complementaries being placed opposite. Adjoining colors are mixed, and the mixtures then have black or white added. There are various other color systems, all of which can form the beginning of exercises. But such experiments, though extremely instructive, should not be carried too far.

Perhaps more suited to the child is the application to a living theme which calls for mixing ('Fishes in Combat' (*Plate 3a*), etc.). The addition of white is particularly important when working on a dark ground or over dark underpainting (see B5).

B5 Painting with Poster Colors on a Colored Ground

Poster colors, including white (see B3), brush (B3), colored paper, thin colored cardboard, or paper painted over.

Gouache (the amount of white will depend on the ground), as described under B4. To experience fully the possibilities of painting in opaque colors, a dark ground is used. A sheet of

a Charcoal Drawing (A 3), 'Landscape,' by a student teacher. Length 28 inches

b Pen Drawing (A4), 'Our Visit to St. Gereon's, Cologne,' by a twelve-year-old boy. Length 25 inches

Plate 3

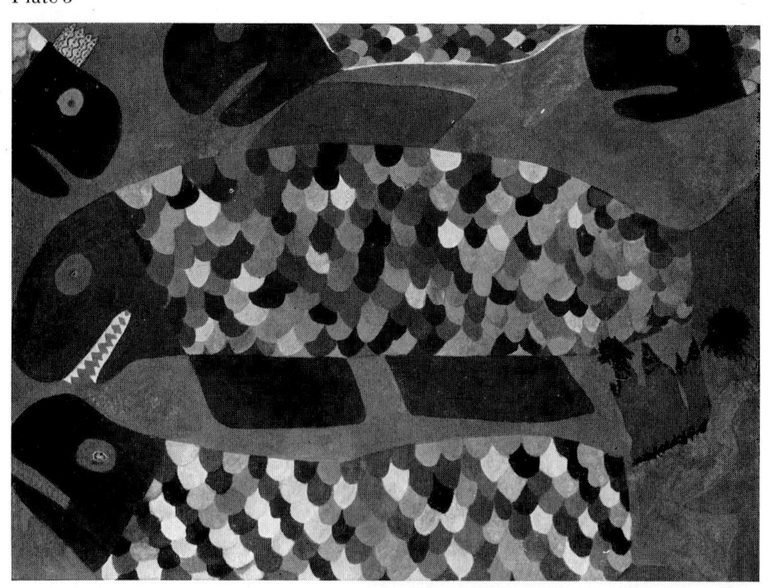

a Gouache with Poster Colors (B3 and B4), 'Fishes in Combat,' by an eleven-year-old boy. Length 24¾ inches

b Outline Painting with Poster Colors (B3b and B 12), 'My Friend and I,' by a twelve-year-old girl. Height 34 inches

a Using a Limited Range of Colors (B6, greens and browns), 'In the Forest,' by a student teacher. Length 27 inches

b Wet Painting and Brush Drawing (B9 and A5), 'Garden' (detail), by a student teacher. Height 18 inches

Plate 5

a Silhouette (D1 and O2), 'Holy Night,' by a group of ten-year-old children. Length 40 inches

b Engraving on Plaster (E5), 'On the Way to School.' $3\frac{1}{2} \times 3\frac{1}{2}$ *inches*

c Engraving on Cardboard (E8), 'Young Cockerels,' by a student teacher. Length 24 inches

paper first painted dark by the pupil will do very well. Only the lighter shades, mixed with white to make them even more opaque, are employed. Any subject in which the darkness is broken up by flashes of light ('Torchlight Procession,' 'Fireworks,' etc.) is suitable (*Plate 13*).

Using a Limited Range of Colors B6

Poster colors, including white; brush as under B3; paper, see A1.

Photographs usually transform colors into black and white. When Matthias Grünewald painted the wings of his Isenheim Altarpiece in grisaille (a gray monochrome underpainting), he did so because he realized the beauty of this technique, and certainly not because he meant to anticipate photography. To practice with a limited range of colors can be of great help to the student. Mixing colors (see B4) becomes inevitable. Practically every subject is suitable, especially if a harmonious effect counts for more than narrative, for example 'Zebras'—gray-in-gray, 'Birds'—shades of blue with touches of silver, 'Giant Grasshoppers'—browns and greens (*Plate 4a*). This technique may appear more suitable for adults, but it can gradually be introduced to children from about the age of eleven, for whom it will even have a special fascination.

Depth and Volume B7

For colors and brushes, see B3; paper, see A1.

The study of depth and volume belongs to the more advanced stages. It is not a problem likely to occupy the teacher of small children. Depth and volume are discussed together, because they set very similar problems, as an example will show. Quite often, even at an early stage, the student may come across intersecting objects, or detail of similar colors, to which he must try to give greater clarity. There may be apples in a basket, sleeves, or the trouser legs of someone shown in profile. The more advanced the pupil, the less he will want to work out contrasts by thick black, or even colored, outlines, much less by entirely arbitrary colors (one red and one blue leg, etc.). By using the same color in varying degrees of light and darkness, a first step is taken towards a more advanced way of modeling, in which the effect of distance is achieved through light and shade. It is also possible, rather than working through chiaroscuro, to employ color variations in a seemingly arbitrary manner to mark the contrast between intersecting objects.

B8 Colored Washes

Poster or watercolors and brushes as under B3; paper as under A1, preferably fairly non-absorbent varieties.

Occasionally, the student may want to add a few colored washes to a pen drawing (see A4 and A5) or even to a pencil or pastel sketch. Quite often, one color (sepia, brown, or gray) will be considered enough. This technique will be suitable only at a more advanced stage. The colors must be applied very thinly, well mixed with water, if they are not to lose their transparency. Under no circumstances must the clarity of the drawing be lost. Though this technique can be used from the age of fourteen onwards, it must never replace 'direct' painting.

B9 Wet Painting

Colors and brushes as under B3, paper as under A1.

Painting on a wet ground has a charm of its own. First of all the sheet of paper has to be dampened on both sides with absolutely clean water, using a sponge, a rag, or even the fingers. A bare table or a drawing board will form an excellent base. It is essential that the paper lie completely flat. The color is then applied in areas or outlines. One may be guided by the flow of the color on the wet paper, or a particular subject ('Trees in the Fog,' 'Magic Flowers,' etc.), which might well come to mind only in the course of painting (see Loosening Techniques, C1 and C4). The paper should not be too wet, or it will be impossible to achieve any form at all, though it has to be kept damp all the time. To know when to stop is important, if the technique is to be more than mere play. A 'wet' picture, when completely dry, can also be used as the basis for tempera (see B3) or a pen or brush drawing (*Plate 4b*).

Watercolor

B10

Watercolors and watercolor brushes, cartridge paper.

Modern educators do not consider watercolor particularly suitable for younger children. Poster colors are generally preferred. Unlike poster colors, watercolors are transparent, *i.e.*, the paper can show through. The floating, almost ethereal effects possible with watercolors—in contrast to the more down-to-earth poster paints—are among the great attractions of this medium. Children and adolescents see little appeal in these qualities, nor does the handling of the technique come easily to the inexperienced. Colors applied in layers often produce all kinds of shades, which only the more advanced students can foresee.

Normally, the ground colors are applied as transparently as possibly over the entire picture. The next stage (overpainting) consists in applying further layers of color to give a feeling of space and volume (see B7). Figures and objects can also be applied directly, rather than developed out of the color. But this is also for the experienced, unless the technique is merely treated as an exercise.

Powder Colors

B11

Powder colors, brush (see B3), as well as a round, long-haired, stiff bristle brush. Any kind of paper (see A1), a small metal palette or bowls.

This technique, which is very popular in England and America, is particularly suitable for children. The small hollows in the palette, or the little bowls, are filled with the required amount of powder color. Since the powder colors already contain the necessary binder, the child merely has to dip the wet brush into the paint without any further mixing, unless it is intended to produce intermediate shades. There will be little waste of material, because the brush will absorb color only while it is wet. The technique is extremely easy to handle; the colors cannot run nor are any other complications likely.

B12 Homemade Poster Colors

Powder colors, paste, round bristle brushes with long bristles, every type of paper, from old newspapers to large sheets of wrapping paper. The technique demands a large format and small pieces of paper should therefore be avoided.

First mix some powder color with a little water, using old tins, etc. The paste—preferably wallpaper paste—having been mixed to a fairly liquid consistency in a larger bowl is then added to the colors in the proportion of one part of paste to five parts of color. The opacity of the colors will depend on the proportion of pigment, water, and paste and can be adjusted according to need.

Bought poster colors, though more expensive, are of far greater luminosity and fastness (*Plate 3b*).

Paint as described under the other techniques (see B3a, b, c and d), possibly using a charcoal or other drawing. The colors are mixed on the palette or in small bowls.

B13 Fresco Painting *(Fresco secco)*

Paste or poster colors (see B12), bristle brush (see B12). Size (optional), plain white wall.

Two coats of size will make a white wall washable. It would thus be possible to let children paint directly on the wall with paste colors, which are easily washed off. In the case of poster colors (most of which become impervious to water after drying) such preparation is unnecessary. In permanent work, the size should be applied over the picture. For making paste colors, see B12. It is advisable to make a preliminary charcoal drawing, which can be treated in the manner described under B3b. Every school ought to have large areas of washable wall for painting; nothing could be more appropriate than decoration carried out by the pupils themselves. Large scale painting by children and adolescents often have a vigor and originality rarely achieved in the work of adults. The technique generally demands subjects involving large figures. If small figures are used in great variety, color should be confined to these, the wall itself being left white. Any suggestion of perspective is to be avoided. This will increase the character of the fresco and will also, in most cases, correspond to new pupils' stage of development.

C LOOSENING TECHNIQUES

C1 Finger Painting

Paste colors (see B12), powder colors (see B11), non-absorbent or water-resistant paper on which the colors will stay wet as long as possible (satin paper).

The prepared color is distributed more or less 'accidentally' over a large area of paper. The pupil now sets to work with his fingers, following entirely his own inspiration. The result may be an abstract or decorative pattern, figures, etc. A completely free play with the colors is fully justified in this case, where the aim is not to produce a picture, but to achieve a loosening effect.

Today, finger painting has its acknowledged place in occupational therapy. But its significance for the healthy child and for art education in general should not be overlooked. The technique has even been used successfully with adults, especially in England and the United States.

C2 Blot Pictures

Any kind of colors soluble in water, any type of paper, tracing pen or ink brush (both optional).

Both Goethe and Leonardo da Vinci said that we should try to see figures in the surface texture of a wall. Our imagination can read form and meaning into almost anything. This ability has been used in connection with all kinds of psychological tests (Rorschach test, etc.).

Homemade blot pictures can be a spur to the imagination in the teaching of art. Pictures can be produced by folding a piece of paper vertically. The sheet is then opened out like a book, and color is splashed on one side of the paper. By closing the pages, we will obtain an almost symmetric blot picture. There are, of course, other ways, such as placing a second sheet on top of our picture, etc. Obviously, all this must be done while the color is still wet.

Now the student can go further and start discovering. The teacher might say to his class: 'Look carefully at your pages. Don't hurry! Can you notice anything? Perhaps you might outline what you see with a pencil so that I can also recognize it. You can work out anything you see as much as you like.' But nothing definite—landscape, animals, figures, etc.—should be suggested. He should speak only in very general terms if the children's imaginations are to unfold fully. It must be understood in this context that one technique does not invalidate another. If the imagination is channeled towards certain limited objectives, perhaps to look only for faces on one occasion or only for landscapes on another, this also has its specific value in art education.

Paste Engravings

C3

Wallpaper paste, drawing ink, writing ink, powder colors, wallpaper brush, non-absorbent or water resistant paper (satin paper).

Having first placed a sheet of paper on newpapers, it is covered with paste using a wide brush (wallpaper brush). The paste, which can be fairly thick, should not be applied too lightly (for making paste, see B12). Then add a little ink (dry powder color, etc.) and set to work again (possibly with another brush). All sorts of pictures can be 'engraved' in the wet paste —which will stay wet for quite a long time—with the hands or with blunt objects like twisted pieces of paper, bits of cardboard, combs, etc. In the course of the work, the light paper ground will become revealed again and again. One can go on and on working, until the paste has dried. Even that moment can be delayed almost indefinitely by adding water from time to time.

C4 Other Loosening Techniques

Loosening techniques, in the teaching of art, are a form of play that aims to release tension in the pupil. All emphasis on 'achievement' and competition is to be avoided. All kinds of materials are suitable, beginning with woolen threads which are allowed to form figures, etc.

As in the Wartegg test, three or more lines of any kind can be drawn on a sheet of paper. The children then start 'interpreting', *i.e.*, evolving forms. Results can be particularly interesting if all the children begin with the same set of lines. All types of seemingly worthless material can be used to help the imagination unfold. Sand, whether in the sandpit or nature, is always an excellent medium, as is everything we find on the ground in a pine forest. Whole landscapes, complete with lakes and mountains, can be built from it.

Old newspapers lend themselves to almost infinite possibilities. They can be folded into the most fantastic animals (no forms should be suggested to the children), made into masks with glued-on paper strips for hair, eyebrows, and beards, or even used for large charcoal drawings.

Other exercises can take the form of games. The children are separated into two or more groups which compete by drawing. At the start, each group sends a representative to the teacher, who whispers a word to him. This word is then demonstrated by drawing—no writing must be used—to the rest of the team, who try to guess its meaning. Whoever guesses it first collects another word, until a certain number has been guessed correctly.

Outline Painting and Filling-in (B 3b). 'Harbor', after Max Pechstein, by a student teacher. Length $23^1/_2$ inches

D SILHOUETTES, etc.

Silhouette

D1

Black (or blackened), white, or colored paper; embroidery scissors (a lino-cutting nib or a razor blade, preferably in a holder, can also be used).

It is best to start on single figures, which are cut out directly without any preliminary drawing. One of the basic rules of the silhouette will soon become clear: there is no perspective, no volume (*Plate 5a*). Even intersections within the figure should be avoided at first. The beginner should concentrate entirely on the clear outline. Paper of any color can be used. Cut either with the scissors or with the cutting nib or razor blade, in which case the paper has to lie flat on a cardboard base. Silhouettes can be made up of separately cut figures, or cut out in one piece.

Later, various forms of piercing can be attempted. At first, a house might be given windows, a dress trimmings. Eventually, even elaborate lace work and tracery will be possible.

If the cutting has been done carefully, there will be no problem in pasting down. Large silhouettes are first placed on the paper to which they are to be stuck, in the right position. Another piece of paper is then put over the lower half of the silhouette and kept in position with a fairly heavy object. The ends of the upper portion are then carefully lifted up, lightly pasted at the back, stuck down, and smoothed out with a sheet of paper. This process is repeated for the lower section.

Folding Cut

D2

Materials as above (D 1).

Folding has almost infinite possibilities. A rectangle can be transformed by vertical folding, a square can be folded diagonally or at right angles. In cutting through all the layers of paper, a variety of patterns may be formed. A certain degree of 'accident' is justified at the early stages, when the pupil can completely surrender to the magic of the technique. Later, with growing experience, he should be able to plan and foresee increasingly. Beginners always incline to cut their forms. At a more advanced stage, one should be able to work in 'relief,' *i.e.*, to obtain the desired form and to cut away the ground. There is no limit to the range of subjects, from the purely geometric and floral design to figure groups. In class work, whole 'tapestries' can be assembled from the work of individual pupils. For pasting down, see D1.

D3 Split Pictures

Materials as above; also textured paper.

In this cutting or tearing technique, the result should be a picture in which the outlines are formed by the ground shining through the pasted-down black or colored paper. The different sections are reassembled as shown in the illustration. A simple start can be made with square or round forms (*Plate 26a*). Possibilities are almost unlimited, from houses and faces to whole groups.

D4 Free Forms

Materials as above. Interesting effects can be achieved with transparent (tracing paper) or textured paper, in white on white, etc.

No limits are set to the pupil's skill or inventiveness. He can design and cut free patterns that somehow hold together, or he can create elaborate arrangements within a 'frame.' Both 'intaglio' and 'relief' are possible, *i.e.*, the forms can be cut away or left standing. Even folding out—particularly suitable in the case of white transparent paper—is not too difficult. Forms can also be cut out separately and grouped later. Deliberate limitation to certain forms is advisable in the case of group work, or if this exercise is used as a party game.

Each type of paper will produce a different effect. For pasting down, see D1.

Shadow-play Figures D5

A firm resilient cardboard (heavy chipboard, old folders, etc.), wire in two thicknesses (a fairly fine wire and one slightly stronger), celluloid strip (optional), scissors.

The figures (in the case of human figures, not less than eight inches high) and stage props are first designed in the manner of silhouettes. Each movable portion is cut again and fitted with a loop, which passes beyond the solid section (the trunk, etc.) to which it is attached with a small spring, which can be formed by twisting a piece of thin wire. The movement mechanism is extremely simple, since only one limb in each figure needs to be mobile. Even in the case of several movable limbs, movement is effected by a system of wires fitted to one arm or leg. The stick for holding each figure (wood, cardboard, or a piece of fairly strong wire) is fitted to the back of a rigid portion. The piece for working the movements (wire, or preferably celluloid strip) is fitted to a movable part, again using wire springs, as in the case of the joints (*Plate 22*).

Shadow-play Stage D6

Wooden battens, tracing paper (about 2 by 5 feet for each scene), black tracing ink or black paper, strip of cardboard, paste.

The stage props (extremely simple and kept to the absolute minimum) are designed in the manner of silhouettes. A certain amount of elaboration, piercing, etc., is quite permissible. Even color may be added by way of transparent paper. One can draw directly on the backcloth (*i.e.*, the sheet of paper) or cut out the figures, etc., and insert them in slits at the sides or the bottom of the stage. The first solution would need a separate sheet of paper for each scene, the second a frame, to which the transparent paper is fitted. It is also possible to paste black or colored silhouettes on transparent paper. The finished stage setting must be shaded by a broad projecting strip of dark paper (such as dark wrapping paper) against the light. If it is to be changeable, it will have to be fitted like a scroll to a piece of wood, which can easily be attached to the framework of the stage. When props have to be added in the course of the play, they are inserted into cardboard pockets at the sides or the bottom of the frame.

The stage can also be improvised from boxes and blankets, or simply by a door opening.

A shadow theater needs a strong source of light (from an epidiascope or similar source).

D7 All-black Drawing

Pen or brush, drawing ink or poster color.

Here, the cut-out silhouette is replaced by a black brush or pen drawing (see D1). The time-honored way of making silhouettes will prove highly suitable: the shadow cast by the sitter on a piece of paper on the wall (a strong source of light is required) is simply traced and filled in with the brush.

E SGRAFFITO AND ENGRAVING

Wax Engraving E1

Wax crayons, cartridge paper (drawing pad), a pen-knife or similar engraving tool.

The first layer of wax is applied all over the paper, using light colors. There is no need to follow any particular design. The second layer is applied in darker colors, until the first is completely covered. The first coat will adhere closely to the paper, while the second can easily be scraped off, revealing the brighter underpainting. The technique is easily handled, even by smaller children, as long as a comparatively small format is used (*Plate 30*).

Mezzotint Technique E2

Fairly non-absorbent paper, white chalk powder, paste, drawing ink, pen-knife or similar engraving tool.

The student prepares the plate himself by covering a sheet of fairly non-absorbent paper with a mixture of chalk powder and paste, which, having dried, is given a coating of black or colored ink. The dry plate can be engraved with a pen-knife, revealing the white ground. All kinds of effects are possible, from a network of delicate lines to broad planes.

Ink Engraving on Gouache or Designers' Colors E3

A fairly non-absorbent paper, gouache or designers' colors, drawing ink, pen-knife or similar engraving tool.

While drawing ink does not adhere to ordinary poster colors (see M5 and M6), it can be applied over certain ready-mixed gouache or designers' colors (Winsor & Newton, Reeves, Arnold), provided these form a sufficiently thick layer, which will be revealed in the process of engraving (see E2). Both undercoat and ink must be completely dry before engraving can start.

E4 A Plaster Picture

Plaster of Paris, a mould (a soup plate or an improvised frame with a glass or linoleum base will serve perfectly), engraving tool (knife, nail, or pin), poster colors, possibly also liquid wax, lacquer, or some other colorless varnish.

The mould can be a plate (see K1), or an improvised batten frame resting on a piece of glass or linoleum. Whatever it may be it first has to be wiped with a damp soapy cloth, so that the cast will not stick. The plaster is then mixed with water in equal proportions in a fairly deep bowl and poured into the form. It will take between ten and twenty minutes to set. (It is advisable to let a few of the children demonstrate the technique of plaster casting in front of the class, leaving the others to do it as a homework task.). A preliminary drawing (nail or pin) will prove of considerable help. The outlined areas are then painted with poster colors. The plaster should be kept slightly damp, or re-dampened if necessary. Younger children ought to be encouraged to paint figures and objects only, and to leave the background white. The same technique can be applied to stone. In general, painting on plaster differs little in character from painting on paper. When the slab has completely dried (on top of a radiator or in a cooking stove, etc.), the picture can be coated with a layer of liquid wax or some colorless varnish, shoe polish, etc. A high gloss can be produced with colorless lacquer. If the picture is to be hung, we merely have to drill a small hole at the back (with a screwdriver or similar implement) as a socket for the nail or picture hook already on the wall.

Engraving on Plaster

E5

Plaster of Paris and mould as under E4, engraving tool (knife, darning needle, etc), drawing ink (also poster colors, colorless varnish).

Plaster engraving has existed in various forms since the earliest days. It is still occasionally used in the decoration of the plasterwork of half-timbered houses in Europe. If properly organized, the technique is quite suitable for classes of children between the ages of eight and fourteen. One of its great advantages is its cheapness. Casting a tile (with a plate or simple improvised frame) has already been described under E4. We can begin as soon as the material has set, when the plaster slab is taken out of its cast. The smooth side, *i.e.*, the side which has adhered to the plate or base, is then covered with black ink or color. When the color has dried—the plaster will take much longer to dry—engraving can start. The fine white lines can be covered with more ink—or the ground color—if absolutely necessary, though corrections should be kept to a minimum (*Plate 5b*). Scraping off larger areas is also possible. Again, a coat of liquid wax or any colorless varnish (see E4) will give a better finish and protect the work.

It must be remembered that this technique largely relies for its effect on the play of the thin white lines and is therefore more suitable for a purely decorative or abstract treatment than for narrative pictures.

Sgraffito

E6

Materials as under E5 (a mixture of sand and paste can be used instead of plaster); fixative spray.

Technique very much like E5, except that the plaster is worked before it has fully hardened. More experienced students who have already done plaster engraving can start engraving in the wet plaster, which has first been sprayed with black ink. Fairly large slabs are preferable, since the effect will be less intricate.

Work must always be done to a prepared design. Beginners will feel safer with a mixture of sand and paste, which takes much longer to dry than plaster—up to several days—and therefore leaves plenty of time for planning and working out detail (for making a sand-and-paste mixture, see E10). As in the case of plaster, the sand-and-paste mixture is sprayed with black ink. White powder paint can be used in mixing to make the sand lighter.

The same technique can be carried out with cement (and white powder paint), which also takes much longer to set than plaster (about 24 hours).

E7 Sgraffito on Underpainting

Materials as under E4.

Technique as under E4, except that the work has as its basis a colored picture painted directly, without drawing, on the plaster or sand-and-paste base. The network of white lines is engraved over the painting, not, however, strictly following the outlines of the figures but emphasizing detail (the feathers of a bird or the scales of a fish, the pointing between bricks, the ribs of leaves, etc.). This filigree-like effect largely accounts for the specific charm of this technique.

E8 Engraving on Cardboard

Blackened cardboard or black poster board, darning needle or sharp knife, etc.

Instead of using white paint or drawing ink on black or dark paper, it is also possible to produce a white line by careful 'engraving.' The drawing, which is not to be followed slavishly, can first be vaguely outlined in pencil, though this is by no means necessary. Thin lines are then formed by a series of dots made with a sharp instrument (darning needle or knife), revealing the white ground (*Plate 5c*). The full possibilities of

Fabric Appliqué (G 4 and O 4), 'Myself with my Scooter', by a group of children, after a design by a thirteen-year-old girl. Height 74 inches

this technique are realized only in the course of the work. Having tried his hand at a small piece, the student can aim at more deliberate effects in a larger task.

Underglass Engraving

E9

Square pieces of glass, opaque colors (poster or oil colors, etc.), engraving tool (pen-knife, darning needle, or nail), gold and silver leaf, oil for mixing (optional).

Underglass engraving is a variation of underglass painting (see M4), an old peasant technique. The pane of glass is first covered, not too thickly, with a layer of black paint (powder color mixed with size in the proportion of one part of color and one part of size to three parts of water). This will produce a surface which is easily engraved. Black poster color can also be used. When the color has dried, the subject can be outlined in pencil or as a white brush drawing. Any suggestion of perspective, distant landscape, etc., would be out of place. Only figures and strictly two-dimensional objects will do justice to this technique. The branches of a small tree would thus appear spread out, without any attempt at intersection. Engraving can be done with a variety of tools (pen-knife, pin, nail, etc.).

Corrections must be carried out with the same material as the ground (drawing ink would affect the ground color and is therefore unsuitable). The picture is then backed with gold or silver paper (any type of gold or silver paper will do) and a piece of cardboard, and edged with gummed tape. In place of a gold or silver backing, the engraving can also be painted in one or several colors. It must be remembered that the picture will be on the back of the pane, *i. e.*, will appear as if it were under glass. A more expensive alternative to gold or silver paper is gold or silver leaf. A special oil has to be used in this case. The gold leaf is applied with a soft brush when the oil has almost completely dried (often not for several days, and only when passing a finger over it produces a slight squeaking sound).

E10 Sand Sgraffito

Sand, powder colors, wallpaper paste, pen-knife, piece of plywood, etc., wooden battens, tins or bowls, etc.

This ancient technique is easily adapted to school use if the sand is mixed with wallpaper paste instead of cement or lime. The resulting mixture, while forming a clean, firm surface, will take much longer to dry and will therefore be simpler to work. Begin by making the portable base. Possible materials include plywood (a sheet not less than 8 by 8 inches), or hardboard. Cardboard, being inclined to buckle when damp, is not suitable. Battens are also needed for a wooden frame. The ready-mixed paste is then added to the dry sand, until a fairly thick mass is formed. Powder colors of a fairly dry consistency will meanwhile have been prepared. No more than four colors, preferably only two or three, should be used. They can be made brighter by adding white. The required quantities of sand mixture are now colored by further thorough mixing. Afterwards they are poured into the form—made from the plywood or hardboard base and the wooden frame—each color forming a flat, comparatively thin separate layer.

Since it will be some time before the layers have hardened sufficiently to become a homogeneous mass there will be ample opportunity to work down to the different colors. The result will be a picture of planes and comparatively thick lines. In making the preliminary design—which is essential—it should be borne in mind that linear effects are more suitable to this technique. The range of subjects is fairly wide, and can include figures, still life, or purely decorative designs.

Work can continue even after the material has hardened. Indeed, in special cases engraving may not start until then.

E11 Plaster Sgraffito

Plaster of Paris, powder colors, mixing bowls, etc., pen-knife.

Layers of colored plaster form an excellent sgraffito base. The mixing and casting of plaster has already been described under E4 (A Plaster Picture). In sgraffito, the plaster first has to be colored. The colors, already mixed in separate bowls or jam jars, are added to the wet and fairly thick plaster mixture, which is then poured into the mould in separate $^1/_8$ inch thick layers, allowing some time for each layer to set—though not harden—before pouring in the next. For the rest, continue as described under E10.

F MOSAIC

F1 Brush Mosaic

Poster colors, etc., flat bristle brush, any kind of paper (large sheets).

Mosaic was already known in antiquity. With certain modification, the technique is easily adaptable to the classroom.

Brush mosaic can either be considered a loosening technique, allowing the children to handle the medium in an 'impressionist' or 'pointillist' manner, or it can become a highly disciplined exercise, based on carefully placed rectangular brush strokes (stiff bristle brush). Any kind of homemade brush, even a rag, will serve in the first case, when the children can work spontaneously without any set task. In the second, the picture is composed of square or rectangular brush strokes—which must be formed directly with the flat brush, and not drawn first in outline with a pointed brush and filled in afterwards—starting with the outlines, or building up the forms from within. The areas left in between are then filled in with further pieces of mosaic, *i.e.*, flat strokes. Great freedom is possible in the use of color. A variety of greens, from near-blue to brown, will add interest to a larger area. The gaps between the 'mosaic' pieces, while quite distinct, must not be too great.

F2 Potato Stamp Mosaic

Raw potato, pen-knife, poster or watercolors, bristle or watercolor brush, a fairly absorbent paper.

Technique as above (F1). Again, a free or a strictly controlled method is possible. For the technique of potato printing, see H1.

Paper Mosaic

F3

Bits of colored paper (any kind), scissors, paste, brush, paper for mounting.

The pupils will usually work to a design, which will also be a guide to the colors. Using bits of colored paper, possibly paper painted by the children themselves, the 'mosaic' pieces are cut out as small squares measuring slightly under $1/2$ by $1/2$ inch. These pieces are then pasted down, working from the outlines of the figure they are to form and leaving tiny gaps, less than $1/16$ inch, between them. In the case of curves, the 'stones' may have to be slightly trimmed (*Plate 9a*).

Note: There are several ways of arranging the mosaic for the more advanced student. The stones can be set in curves parallel to the outline, to introduce movement, or they can be arranged along a vertical-horizontal axis throughout the whole figure. By using several methods in the same picture, the contrast between the different portions will become more marked. A slight change in areas of the same color also adds interest. Even the introduction of small pieces of an entirely different color is permissible.

Mosaic with Natural Materials

F4

Sand, pebbles, pine-needles, grass, leaves, etc.

Working with natural materials, with the earth as a base, is a very suitable introduction to more elaborate forms of mosaic. In being left to work exactly as they like, the children will discover certain basic laws of this technique.

But it is also possible to work to set tasks. The size of the area might be clearly defined, or some sort of subject might be given ('A Horseman,' 'Old Witch,' etc.).

Mosaic on Clay

F5

Clay (also plasticine, etc.), colored sands, pebbles, etc.

The technique resembles that described under F4, though it demands a little more skill owing to the smaller base, made by the pupil himself. Normally, subjects will be confined to figures, beginning with the outlines, while the background is left bare. Because of its high water content, clay requires a firm base (plywood, hardboard, etc.). Plasticine, as well as many brands of modeling clays, can be used again and again.

F6 Mosaic on a Sand-and-Paste Base

Sand, wallpaper paste, bits of stone for mosaic (for making plaster mosaic, see F8) or colored pebbles, broken tiles, etc.

For making a sand-and-paste mixture and a mould for the base, see E10. Having poured the mixture (possibly colored, see E10), which need not be absolutely smooth, into the mould setting the mosaic begins. Since the paste takes a long time to set, there is no need to hurry. Start with the outlines, using stones whose color contrasts strongly with that of the base (bits of plaster mosaic, see F8, are particularly suitable because of their brilliant colors). The stones are set closely, though not entirely adjoining. Throughout, care must be taken to achieve sufficient contrast in the colors of the figures. Large forms will suit this technique best. It is usually unnecessary to fill the entire ground. Figures will generally stand out much better against the plain base (*Plate 32*).

This technique is particularly suitable for schools. It is fairly clean, there is little to spoil that cannot be put right in the course of the work, and it lends itself to the making of pictures in brilliant lasting colors.

F7 Mosaic on Cement

Cement, sand, stones, as above; also bits of colored and transparent glass, etc.

Technique as above, but using cement instead of paste in the proportion of one part of sand to one part of cement. Having mixed the ingredients with water to a fairly thick consistency, this is poured into the mould (see F6), or even into a provisional batten frame resting on a linoleum or glass base (*Plate 9c*). For setting the mosaic, see F6.

Pieces of colored glass—possibly colored by the children—can also be used. Set at an angle projecting above the cement, they will produce an interesting three-dimensional effect.

There is another method of using glass. Cut the glass with the glass cutter into strips slightly under 1/2 inch in width and insert these into the cement sideways, using pieces of any length. The figures are again built up from the outlines, working inwards. By giving the strips different directions, a remarkable degree of articulation is possible throughout. By alternative flat and projecting strips, the picture can be given startling light effects. The glass will be firmly embedded in the hardened cement (*Plate 15b*).

Colored Plaster Mosaic (Stucco)

F8

Plaster of Paris, powder colors soluble in water, wallpaper paste, glass or linoleum base, wooden battens, bristle brush, spoon, two mixing bowls, handsaw, pen-knife, nails, hammer.

a. Making the colored plaster mosaic pieces

First the powder color has to be mixed, using very little water. The base (glass or linoleum) is then given a very thin coating of soap as an insulating layer. Now the plaster can be prepared, using water and plaster in equal quantities. The plaster is put by the spoonful into the other mixing bowl—which has been half filled with water—until it forms a small mound. Only then can a start be made on the mixing, taking care to obtain a smooth paste, to which the prepared color mixture is added in the desired quantity. Then the paste is stirred again. The whole process must be well prepared and must not take too long, since plaster sets very quickly (within ten minutes). The colored paste is poured on the prepared base and spread out with a broad knife or spatula to a thickness of 1/4 inch. While the plaster is still setting, make horizontal and vertical cuts, forming mosaic pieces slightly under 1/2 inch square. When the plaster has fully hardened, these can be detached from their base with a spatula without any difficulty.

b. Setting the mosaic

A pane of glass is given a thin coating of soap, as above. It may help the work in some cases if the glass, soapy side up, is placed over the design. The mosaic stones, smooth side down, are now pasted to the glass with a bristle brush, using very little paste. It is most important that only adhesives soluble in water should be used. As before, it is advisable to begin with the outlines. The stones should not be placed too closely (see F6), leaving very narrow, though noticeable, gaps. Where necessary they are slightly trimmed. There is no need to set the entire picture in mosaic, since the plaster, which is poured in afterwards, and which will in any case hold all the stones in position, can form the background to the figures. But before pouring in the fairly liquid plaster mixture a provisional frame will be needed. This is placed on top of the sheet of glass to prevent the plaster flowing in all directions. Having poured in the plaster, possibly in several layers, depending on the size of the pane (a pane one foot square will require a layer of plaster slightly under an inch thick), it is necessary to wait for the plaster to harden completely (up to an hour) before the plaster slab can be detached first from the frame, and then from the sheet of glass or linoleum (*Plate 32*).

It will take several days for the last traces of water to evaporate completely, when a thin coating of wax can be applied. By polishing the waxed picture, the colors are restored, which until then will have appeared somewhat dull, to their original glow. Size, a good substitute for wax polish, helps to produce a high gloss if applied under the wax or colorless varnish.

a 'The Three Kings', by a group of three twelve-year-old children. Height 22 inches

b Paper Appliqué (G 1), 'Red Indian', by an eleven-year-old boy. Height 23½ inches

Other Types of Plaster Mosaic F9

Materials as above.

a. With white outlines

Use only white plaster mosaic pieces (or white chalk, cut to the required size with a sharp knife), forming an outline drawing. Colored plaster (perhaps black or some dark color) is then poured in (see F8). The result is a colored slab with a white mosaic drawing.

b. Inlay

As above, but with two different plaster mixtures, one for the figures inside the mosaic outline and one for the background. To save material, form only a very thin layer of colored plaster, and then pour the white mixture over the entire work.

c. Using additional materials

As above. The mosaic outline (perhaps also a few freely distributed pieces of mosaic within) acts as a wall between the areas of colored plaster, preventing the wet mixture from overflowing. Interesting effects can be obtained by adding sand, dry powder color, chalk, or even metal dust before pouring in the white plaster.

d. With other materials, retaining the plaster base

Pieces of brick, broken tiles, colored or plain glass, etc., can be used instead of plaster mosaic. Plaster can still serve as the binding medium, though cement, mortar, concrete, or even clay, will suit equally well (*Plate 15b*).

Transparent Glass Mosaic F10

Colored glass fragments (used flat), pane of glass for the base, transparent adhesive, putty, glass cutter.

The pane of glass, which acts as the base, is placed over the design. The pieces of glass are then attached with transparent adhesive to the pane, following the sketch underneath. Where necessary, the glass is trimmed with the glass cutter. The seemingly arbitrary changes, caused by the irregular shapes of the pieces of glass, and particularly noticeable when the picture is used as a transparency, are among the most charming effects produced by this technique. There is no need to lay out the entire picture in colored glass. Joins and dividing lines can be filled with putty.

Variation: Fragments of colored glass panes—as distinct from broken bottle glass, which is not suitable in this particular case—are not always easily obtained. Transparent paper will form an excellent substitute (*Plate 10b*). Proceed as above. A paper transparency produced in this technique is no imitation of a stained glass window with black lines between areas of color. It follows its own laws, exploiting to the full the possibilities of the material.

G APPLIQUÉ AND TEXTILE TECHNIQUES

Paper Appliqué

G1

Colored papers of any kind (including used wrapping paper), brown paper as a base, wallpaper paste or any paste soluble in water, scissors, bristle brush, etc.

Working with colored papers directly or with designs (the child's own drawings) is a technique highly suitable for children and can be started at an early age. The paper is cut out or torn to the shape of the desired objects and pasted to a neutral base (wrapping paper, etc.). No background effects (such as landscape) should be attempted. The first layer of appliqué can be further elaborated. Trimmings can be pasted to a dress, windows stuck on a building can have a layer of tracery superimposed, etc. (*Plate 8b*).

Wallpaper Collage

G2

Wallpaper fragments, cartridge paper, etc., also old newspapers, wallpaper paste, scissors, paste brush.

If wallpaper fragments are used in the manner described under G1 it is because even wallpapers of no great merit add interest to a collage. The technique somehow seems to offset inferior designs. Many outstanding modern painters, among them Picasso, have created vast pictures in wallpaper collage. The student should confine himself to subjects involving large figures. The paper can be cut or torn. Old newspapers should be used to protect the work during pasting.

Transparent Paper Appliqué

G3

Both colored and colorless transparent paper (tracing paper, as used by draughtsmen, is particularly suitable), scissors, brush, transparent adhesive.

Technique as above, but using a transparent ground (tracing paper, possibly framed), keeping in mind that the work is meant to be a transparency (to be hung up against the window or some other source of light). The adhesive will have to be used very sparingly for the same reason. This technique, which is chiefly suitable for the older age groups, relies for effect entirely on the fall of the light through the varying thicknesses of transparent paper. The most enchanting results can be obtained, especially when the student is confined to colorless paper (*Plate 10b*).

One can also cut out figures in part only, folding out the rest. This method allows many variations, among them the introduction of additional layers of paper.

G4 Fabric Appliqué

a. Pasting

Fabric remains (plain or patterned, though not too thick), wrapping paper as a base, wallpaper paste, scissors, wide bristle brush, newspapers for working on.

In this technique, the pieces of material are treated as colors, which are pasted on wrapping paper by way of 'painting.' Children will enjoy working in this manner, particularly if they are allowed to explore its possibilities without, at first, any set task. Patterned fabrics provide in themselves a source of inspiration. Thin materials are to be preferred, since they are generally easier to paste down. Proceed as under G1, pasting the material at the back. Those who feel reluctant to use paste on textiles can join the appliqué with a few simple stitches. But there can be no real objection to pasting, as long as the work is purely 'non-functional' and confined to materials of little value (*Plate 7*).

b. Sewing

Fabric remains as above, scissors, needle, darning cotton.

Technique as above, except that a fabric base is used, sewn from odd bits of material or of one piece, in place of wrapping paper. Then sew on the pieces of appliqué, possible working to a previous design, with a special type of stitch (herringbone stitch, etc.).

Weaving Pictures on an Improvised Loom

G5

Wooden battens, hammer and nails (for the loom), darning cotton, thin string for the warp threads, fabric remains (cut into narrow strips), wool, etc., for the weft (grass, or straw, etc., can be used in place of wool).

To make the loom, nail the four battens together so that they form a square or rectangular frame. Then insert an equal number of nails halfway at two opposite sides at distances of about $^1/_2$ inch. The warp threads must be firmly stretched, looped over the nails, and tied up either in pairs to form a fringe, or only at the corners. The strips of material (not more than $^3/_4$ inch wide) are inserted directly by hand, without the help of a shuttle or shed stick, etc. Each weft thread is pressed firmly against the preceding one and 'shaped' to the right and left, making sure that the 'carpet' is of an even width throughout. When forming colored figures (parallel to the warp chains), remember that there will be vertical slits between areas of different color (Kelim technique) unless one goes round the entire warp thread or inserts the new piece through the loop formed by the old (Gobelin technique) (*Plate 10a*).

Embroidery on Canvas

G6

Canvas (stretched on an improvised frame), colored wools, darning needle.

Embroidered wall hangings worked on canvas were already known in the Middle East in the early Middle Ages.

The design is outlined on the canvas in ordinary or drawing ink. Adjoining areas of color are then worked in cross stitch. This will require a certain degree of planning, depending on the subject. Improvised stitches only lead to waste of material. The entire canvas is embroidered, leaving nothing of the ground to show through.

G7 Embroidery on Linen

Linen ground (also other plain materials such as cotton, etc.), colored yarns, possibly wool, darning needle.

Free embroidery on stiff paper can begin at an early age and will form an excellent introduction to more elaborate work.

The material first has to be stretched. A homemade batten frame is perfectly adequate. Each theme may require a different type of stitch. Let the children invent freely, and suggest only that they might begin with faint lines, following the forms of the figures, or work out an area in stitches invented by themselves, always aiming at an uncomplicated picture. Whole areas can be 'painted' in this manner, introducing a note of variety through changes in color. The background should remain empty. Here, as in other techniques, materials used sparingly will generally produce better results.

G8 String or Thread Appliqué

a. Pasting

Paper, wrapping paper, cardboard, etc., for the base; fairly thick string, adhesive.

Place the string on the cardboard ground, forming either a design or figures. In pasting down, the cord can be cut at the points of crossing over, unless it is intended to take advantage of the intersections by deliberate repetition.

Plain string will look better on a colored ground, colored

string on a white ground. In special cases, sections of the string or the ground might be dyed different colors.

b. As Embroidery

As above, except that the string is secured with stitches on a textile ground, which may consist of pieces sewn together by the pupils. An improvised wooden frame will be required. The string can again be colored, though natural string can look particularly effective against a dark ground. Instead of using a picture frame, the embroidery can be hung on the wall with wooden rings or fabric loops, through which a wooden rod can be passed which is hung up by a suitable cord.

c. As a thread picture

A drawing in white thread is sewn onto a black cardboard ground. It is important to sew directly, and not to work from a prepared drawing. The technique must be allowed to produce its own kind of expression. This will mean straight lines and rather 'abstract' subjects.

Leather Appliqué and Leather Pictures G9

Odd pieces of leather, cardboard, or similar ground, adhesive (cold glue, etc.), needle and thread (if used as a hanging).

Small pieces of colored leather, trimmed and placed in exactly the right position on top of a carefully prepared design, using a strong adhesive, can form a type of inlay that seems particularly suited to the character of this material. Leather pictures for hanging on the wall are made by joining the separate pieces with strong thread in herringbone stitch. To avoid buckling, larger pictures have to be made in sections, which are joined later.

H PRINTING AND TRACING TECHNIQUES

H1 Potato Stamps

Raw potato, pen-knife, poster colors, bristle or watercolor brush, a fairly absorbent paper.

The simplest means of duplicating is the stamp. Potato stamps are easily made by cutting into the end of a firm potato, leaving the intended form (star, circle, etc.) to stand out in relief. The poster color is then applied and the potato is used like an ordinary rubber stamp. Whole friezes can be developed from one or two designs. Colored papers of every kind, book covers, and even wallpapers are within the scope of this technique. The finished work is made waterproof with a light coating of beeswax (also floor polish or candle grease) and polished with a brush or soft rag. See also F2, Potato Stencil Mosaic.

H2 Cardboard Stamps

Cartridge paper or thin cardboard, scissors, printing ink, tissue paper, small rubber roller, small pane of glass, paper knife (optional).

This technique is a particularly cheap and simple form of relief printing, *i.e.*, printing with the raised portions of the block or stamp, in contrast to intaglio printing (etching, woodcut, etc.) in which the print is produced by the color in the incised lines. Here, the 'block' is virtually a silhouette, made for easier handling from cardboard or cartridge paper (see D1). Before applying the ink with a roller, the block is placed on a few sheets of newspaper. The printing ink is then transferred from the pane of glass to the block, which, having been inked, is put on a sheet of clean newspaper, inked side up. Now the absorbent paper is put over it, pressed down, and smoothed out. The work is easily controlled by raising the corner slightly. The

a Paper Mosaic (F3 and O3), 'A Fire,' by a group of thirteen-year-old children. Length 50 inches

b Appliqué Chalk Drawing (G1 and B2), 'Cockerel in the Sun' (detail, 4 inches long), by a five-year-old girl

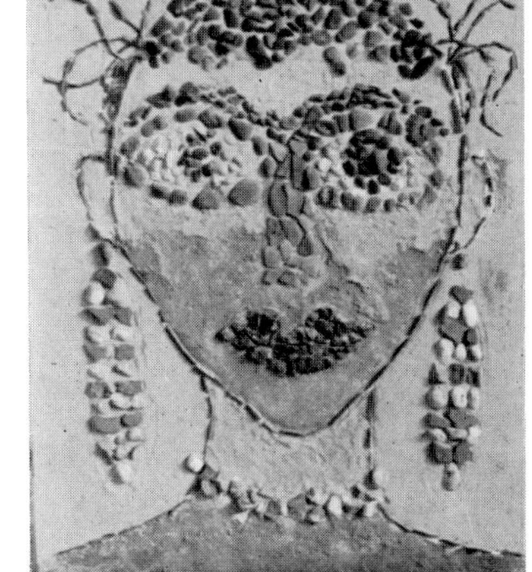

c Mosaic on Cement (F7, pebbles and brick fragments), 'Gypsy Woman,' by a fourteen-year-old girl. Height 28 inches

a Weaving Pictures on an Improvised Loom (G5), 'Nursery Rug,' by a fourteen-year-old girl. Length 32 inches

b Folding Cut in Transparent Paper (F10 and G3), 'Ships,' by a student teacher. Length 20 inches

a Lino Print (H5), 'Man Playing Violin,' by an eleven-year-old boy. Length 18 inches

b Soft Pencil Lino Rubbing (H6), 'Man Playing Violin,' by an eleven-year-old boy. Length 18 inches

a A Lino Stencil as a Picture (H7 and H10), 'Carnival,' by a twelve-year-old boy. Length 19 inches

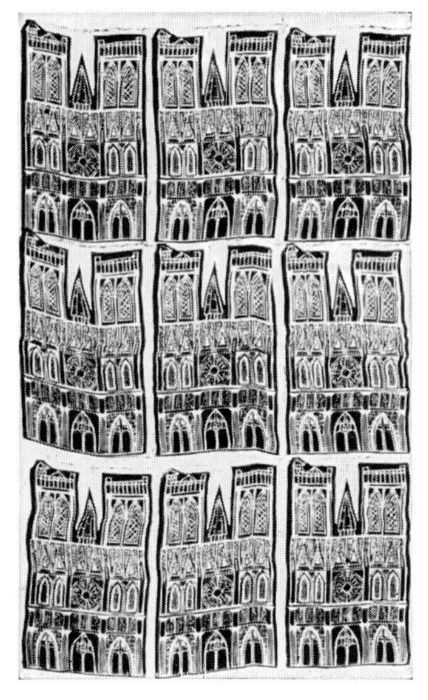

b Lino Bronze Print (H8, gold on dark violet), 'Carnival,' by a twelve-year-old boy. Detail, length 19 inches

c Fabric Printing (H9), 'Wall Hanging for an Assembly Hall,' by a fifteen-year-old boy. Length 72 inches

d Fabric Printing (H9, two colors), 'Wall Hanging for a Nursery,' by an eleven-year-old boy. Width 44 inches

equipment can be cleaned afterwards with turpentine or turp substitute, or with any of the proprietary fluids supplied for this purpose.

Stencil Printing

H 3

Thin board, scissors, brush, poster colors (also writing or drawing ink), any kind of absorbent paper.

Stencil printing is a variation of the technique described under H2, except that the subject will appear as a negative against the colored ground. The stencil is pressed against the paper with the left hand, while the right guides the brush over the stencil and the surrounding area. All kinds of groupings, even intersections, are possible. Indeed, any subject involving massed figures is suitable.

Spray Printing

H 4

Cardboard or strong drawing paper (possibly absorbent paper), scissors, drawing ink, fixative spray or a sieve, an old toothbrush, pins.

This is another variation of the technique described under H3, except that the stencil is secured to the paper with pins. Then spray, using a fixative spray, one end of which is immersed in the liquid, or a toothbrush and a sieve, to which drawing ink has been applied with a brush. The ink having dried, remove the stencil. The result will be a white area on a black ground. Since the stencil will also have become black in the process, it can be used very effectively to contrast with the white negative, perhaps in a chequer board design which incorporates the work of the whole class (see O2, Joining Individual Contributions).

Lino Printing

H 5

Plain linoleum, linoleum cutters, printing ink, rubber roller, small pane of glass, absorbent paper, paper knife (optional).

There are few problems with this technique, as long as the pupil is aware of the simple rules set out below:

a. White outlines: Instead of drawing a design on paper, cut directly into the linoleum with the linoleum-cutter. The result after printing will be a white drawing on black ground.

b. Black figures on a white ground: If the area around the figures outlined as under (a) is cut away with a U-shaped gouge so that it cannot print, black figures on a white ground will be obtained (*Plate 31*).

c. White figures on a black ground: Similarly, white figures on a black ground can be produced if the drawing is not too intricate. The ground is left standing, and most of the area of the figures, except for the raised lines, is scraped off (*Plate 11a*).

All kinds of variations are possible, though it must be understood that too much perspective, intersections, etc., are not really suitable for this technique (*Plates 12c and 12d*). For printing, see H2.

H6 Lino Rubbings

Lino cut (see H5), soft pencil or red chalk, oil crayons, etc., a fairly soft paper.

Children enjoy making coin rubbings from an early age (*Plate 11b*). Lino cuts can be treated in the same way. The paper is placed on top of the cut, being held carefully in position, and gone over with the pencil. Experimenting with different kinds of paper will yield interesting results.

H7 Lino Monotype

Lino cut (see H5), printer's ink in various colors (black, red, brown, etc.), rubber roller, small pane of glass, paper as under H5, paper knife, turp substitute.

Instead of coating the linotype with one color, the student can apply several layers, each being different. This will produce several intermediate shades (the roller can be cleaned between applying layers, though this is by no means essential). The student can also substitute poster colors for printer's ink. These are similarly applied with the brush, though they can be allowed to dry completely, since a slightly damp and absorbent paper is used for printing. The block itself can also be used as a picture (see H10; also *Plate 12a*).

Lino Bronze Print

H8

Lino cut (see H5), red or yellow printer's ink (possibly students' oil colors as a substitute), gold or silver bronze powder, rubber roller, small pane of glass, black absorbent paper, paper knife, etc., turp substitute.

This technique is like any other form of relief print (see H2). Gold and silver are particularly effective on a black ground. First an ordinary print is made, preferably in red or yellow, though other colors will do. While the color is still damp, the bronze powder is dusted over it. Tapping against the print from below makes sure that the metal dust is evenly distributed. The surplus is removed if necessary with a soft watercolor brush after drying (*Plate 12b*).

Fabric Printing (Repeat patterns)

H9

A stamp cut from a cork or a lino cut (up to four inches and above in diameter), piece of soft material, fabric printing colors, rubber roller, small pane of glass.

The technique resembles that of the stamp print (see H1) and of the lino cut (see H5). The piece of material is stretched on a table over several layers of newspaper. The places to be printed can then be marked with chalk (*Plates 12c and 12d*). Smaller designs are applied by covering the block with a piece of thick wood of roughly the same size, and hitting it with carefully aimed hammer blows; in the case of larger designs go over them with a rolling pin which allows for even distribution of the pressure. (For designs, see H5.)

H10 Transforming a Lino Cut into a Picture

Used lino cut, powder color, paste or glue, etc., bronze varnish.

A used lino cut can be turned into an attractive picture, provided its lines are clean and disciplined (see H5). A thinned bronze varnish (bronze powder thinned with turp substitute) is painted over the entire block and afterwards wiped off with a soft rag. The gold will thus be concentrated in the sunken portions, though a faint trace might be allowed to remain on the raised areas.

Chalk bound with paste, etc., can take the place of bronze powder. The technique will be the same. To bring out the picture more strongly, a roller with printing ink can be passed over it after the layer of paste-bound color has dried (*Plate 12a*).

H11 Glass Monotype

Small pane of glass, printer's ink, bristle brush (optional), rubber roller, absorbent paper (sugar paper, the back of old wallpaper, etc.).

Spread the printer's ink on the glass with finger, brush, or roller. Then draw in the ink with a piece of wood—the handle of the brush, etc.—or cardboard. To take the print, a sheet of paper is placed over the glass, pressed against it, and carefully pulled off.

H12 Reverse Printing

Small pane of glass or cardboard (hardboard, etc.), oil colors (one or several), rubber roller, paper.

The color is applied to the sheet of glass or cardboard, etc., with the rubber roller, as for preparing a lino print or wood cut (H5). When the color is fairly—but not completely—dry, a piece of paper can be placed over it. At this stage, the paper will not absorb any of the color without further aid, though this will vary considerably, depending on the kind of paper. Lines, or even areas, can then be impressed on the paper from above, using the fingers or some kind of implement. In the process, the color will have been transferred from the base to the sections of the paper to which pressure has been applied. Several colors can be used, either in layers on one pane, or separately.

Cardboard Engraving (Intaglio)

H 13

A strong cardboard (such as heavy chipboard), paper knife, black printer's ink, rubber roller, small pane of glass, a fairly absorbent paper (see H5).

A drawing is made on a piece of cardboard, using the paper knife. Printer's ink applied to the cardboard (see H2) will not reach the sunken areas, and the picture obtained after printing (see H2) will therefore show a white drawing against the dark ground (*Plate 14a*).

Drypoint

H 14

Zinc plate, etc. (a piece of thin sheet metal or celluloid will form an excellent substitute) about $^1/_{32}$ inch thick, etching needle or a nail, etc., printer's ink (in the case of a relief print the type used for copper engraving, prints being taken in the copper print press; for intaglio prints, see H13), absorbent paper (see H5).

Technique as under H13, except that the material worked is harder. In a drypoint, the drawing is obtained by the metal shavings at the side of the furrow. Relief prints can be taken only in a special printer's press. The color, in that case, is applied only to the grooves, though some will adhere to the burrs (*Plate 14c*). For taking an intaglio print, see H2. In one possible variation (see H7) of the relief print, print in two colors, first with the plain and then with the engraved plate. The effect will not be unlike an intaglio print.

H15 Thread Printing

Thread, cardboard, quick-drying adhesive, scissors, rubber roller, printer's inks, absorbent paper (tissue or sugar paper, etc.).

The only things needed are a piece of string of any thickness (though only one thickness per block), cardboard, and adhesive. One should be guided entirely by the material, and not by any preliminary drawing. Intersections, etc., should be avoided. If absolutely inevitable, the string can be cut and re-set, otherwise the block will be of different heights throughout, which would make printing almost impossible. When the string has set—a wide range of subjects is possible, from purely decorative designs to figures—the color is applied as under H2 or H5, touching only the raised areas. For printing, see H2 and H5. A particularly interesting effect can be obtained by rhythmic repetition of one or two motives (*Plate 14b*).

J SCULPTURE IN THE ROUND

Making Figures from Odd Materials J1

Horse chestnuts, acorns, match boxes, spent matches, glass beads, wire, thread, bits of wood, odd bits of material, paper, cardboard, cigarette boxes, silver paper, tin foil, feathers, etc., pen-knife.

Here, the aim is to let the imagination unfold without any restraint. Animals and people, houses and trees, monsters and machines of every kind, and even purely abstract compositions are all within the possibilities of this technique. It would therefore be out of place to give more than the most general directions in the use of the materials. The principal tool will be the pen-knife. To make the utmost of the character of each material, all adhesives, etc., should be avoided. Joining can be done entirely by slits and insertions. If the results are sometimes unforeseen this is all the better.

Folding and Cutting J2

Stiff paper, thin cardboard, corrugated paper or tin (old tin cans, scissors, metal scissors, fretsaw (possibly metal saw).

The children can work to certain rules in the form of a game:

1. Only cardboard strips of the same width, though of any length, are to be used. By horizontal and vertical creases, slits and insertions, three-dimensional structures can be created both abstract or naturalistic and entirely in keeping with the character of this material.

2. The intended object or figure is to be cut in one piece from a fairly large sheet of cardboard. There is to be no joining, the final three-dimensional result being achieved by bending and folding. All the possibilities of paper cutting are to be exploited to the utmost (rows of teeth, hair, spirals, etc.).

3. The results are to be obtained by folding rather than cutting. Almost any kind of paper can be used (see also L7).

J3 Wire Sculpture

All kinds of wire, pliers.

This technique offers many possibilities. A four-legged animal can be made out of one piece of wire in an unbroken line, or the set task might be an abstract composition, balanced on three legs, the more intricately the better (*Plate 15a*). Or again, the student can try as many ways of joining wire, even the smallest pieces, as he can imagine.

J4 Plaster Sculpture on a Wire Frame

Materials as above, plaster mixing bowl.

This represents a further stage of wire sculpture. The frame need be no more than an indication of the final form. Where curves are desired, newspaper or brown paper can be wound around the frame and secured with thin wire. The plaster mixture, which should be fairly thin, about the consistency of cream, is then applied with the fingers (see E4). Only as much plaster as can be used in one application should be mixed at a time. Gradually a layer of about 1/4 to 1/2 inch can thus be built up. The rough surface has a beauty of its own. If it is to be smoothed, this can be done with the wet hand in the course of the work. The finished sculpture can be painted in any colors soluble in water. A final coat of varnish, size, etc., will make it more durable.

J5 Tin Sculpture

Very thin sheet metal (also old tin cans, etc.), metal scissors, possibly also hammer, pliers, nails, and wire.

Painting with Poster Colors on a Colored Ground (B 5), 'A Fairy Tale', by an eleven-year-old boy. Height 22 inches

One possible task might be to make a small standing animal figure out of a small square of tin—perhaps cut from an old tin can—entirely by cutting into and folding, without trimming off and discarding any of the material. It is also possible to make an animal in parts and to join them by slits and insertions. If absolutely necessary, small pieces of wire, to be inserted through holes made with a nail, can be used. Though imagination and the gift for improvisation should not be unduly restrained, there must always be insistence on clean and careful work.

Modeling

J6

Plasticine, etc., glitter-wax, potter's clay.

While the younger child should be allowed to draw or model freely, the older age group ought to be accustomed to definite tasks (*Plate 16a*).

The purely technical side presents few difficulties. Unfortunately, there is still very little creative modeling practised in schools. This is due chiefly to a general lack of understanding of the inner needs of the child. Little change can be expected there until handwork is considered more than a preliminary stage to a future occupation.

Plasticine and glitter-wax, etc., unlike potter's clay, are clean and can be used again and again. Most catalogues of educational suppliers also list a number of other modeling materials which are often cheap and pleasant to handle.

Plaster and Slag Block Carving

J7

(a) Plaster of Paris, cardboard, wood or glass for the base (see below), pen-knife.

(b) Slag block, handsaw, hammer, rasp, file, etc.

a. Plaster carving

First make a plaster slab of the required size. For a small

figure this will measure about $2^1/_2$ by 3 by 5 inches. The lid of a cardboard box, its sides strengthened with battens to stop them bulging while the plaster sets (about 10 minutes) will do, though a wooden box—a seedbox, etc.—is preferable. Unless the gaps between the boards are very wide the plaster mixture is not likely to escape through them.

Carving can begin immediately after the plaster has set. Plaster is always easier to carve while it is still damp. Work either directly or from a drawing vaguely outlined in the plaster. Forms should be large and simple. If, in polishing, the entire surface is easily reached with a piece of sandpaper, one can be sure that excessive detail has been avoided.

b. Slag Block Carving

Recently, slag blocks—to be obtained from builder's merchants—have been used more and more in craftwork (*Plate 26c*). It is material worked similarly to plaster, with a pleasant texture and color.

J8 Woodcarving

Any kind of wood—pieces of any size, sharp knife, possibly a chisel, etc., rasp, sandpaper.

For technique, see J7. Larger pieces have to be placed into a vice or G-clamp. Softwoods (pine, fir, etc.), because of their grain and structure, are not suitable for more elaborate work. The utmost advantage should be taken of the natural beauty of the material. Each variety will allow a different treatment. Color, if used at all and only to emphasize detail, should be kept to the absolute minimum.

J9 Masks from Paper Bags

Large paper bags, bits of wool, odd pieces of material, grass, etc., scissors, poster colors and brush, adhesive.

A large paper bag, big enough to go over the head, can be developed into a mask by painting, making slits for eyes (perhaps only one opening for a particularly weird 'cyclopean' mask), nose and mouth (*Plate 15c*) and the addition of tusks, paper teeth, and beards from scraps of wool, etc. Groups of masked performers, robed in gray blankets or colored bed spreads and moving to a simple rhythm, accompanied by the simplest music (saucepan lids, rattles, etc.), never fail to impress.

Papier-mâché Puppets

J 10

Newspaper, wallpaper paste, old bottles or cardboard tubes as supports, poster colors, plasticine, handsaw.

a. Solid Heads

The papier-mâché mixture for the head is made by soaking pieces of newspaper about four inches square in medium thick wallpaper paste, kneading them carefully, and freeing them of all surplus moisture by thorough squeezing. When forming the head, over the end of the cardboard tube or the neck of the bottle, always begin with the neck, which has to be hollow (for inserting the finger) and must have a ridge at the base for attaching the clothes. Then press in the hollow for the eyes and shape the nose. Lips, chin, and ears follow. With the rest of the head, they will determine the character of the puppet (*Plate 16b*). Afterwards, a final layer of tissue paper can be applied and smoothed with wallpaper paste. This will also make painting easier. The general effect should be accentuated, even exaggerated, by color.

b. Hollow Heads

Very large heads are easier to handle if they are made hollow over a clay or plasticine head, which is covered with about ten layers of newspaper cut in strips and soaked in wallpaper paste. Each layer is carefully smoothed down to follow the shape of the head. When the head has completely dried, it is cut in two above the ears (not symmetrically down the nose, or the join will show), the core is removed, and the two portions are stuck together with gummed tape. A cardboard tube (or a stick in the case of stick puppets) is then glued into the hole in the neck for the finger.

c. Puppet Theaters

The puppet's clothes are easily made from square pieces of material. The index finger is inserted in the hollow in the neck, the other fingers go into the sleeves. A blackboard or an arrangement of desk and woolen blankets will make an adequate stage. A stage can also be made from battens and brown paper. It could consist of a backdrop and two folding wings, which would also give it better support. No limits are set to the imagination in regard to decor, curtains, or lighting, etc.

K RELIEF TECHNIQUES

Plaster Relief

K 1

Plaster of Paris, mould (see E4 and J7; a soup plate will do), pen-knife (or lino cutting tool, see H5), possibly size or liquid wax for varnishing.

A soup plate, the inside wiped with a soapy rag, can serve as a mould. The coating of soap is necessary to allow for detaching the cast (see F8). If the cast should adhere very firmly, it is gradually worked loose with a knife along the edge.

Carving begins as soon as the plaster has set (either side can be carved). Work in three stages:

1. Line drawing (see H5). An incised plaster drawing can be used for printing like a lino cut. The drawing is made with the tip of a knife or a lino cutting tool. All three-dimensional effects, intersections, etc., should be avoided, the figures being clearly distributed over the whole area in the manner of silhouettes.

2. The outlines can then be deepened; the suggestion of further rounding the drawing into relief will seem obvious. As yet, the ground is left standing.

3. Finally, the ground between the figures can also be cut into, thus making the relief stand out clearly.

But this technique offers many other possibilities, of which one can become fully aware only by experiment.

Slate Relief

K 2

Pieces of roofing slate, pen-knife.

First draw on the slate in pencil. Large and substantial forms—'Elephant,' 'Crocodile,' even faces or the human form in profile—are more suitable than thin and elaborate ones. The pencil drawing is then retraced with the pen-knife, gradually deepening the incised outline. Eventually, the knife will be held almost horizontally. The final result will be a figure highest in the middle and lowest towards the outlines, an effect not unlike that of a small hill rising from a moat (*Plate 27a*). The ground between the figures is left standing. Since the scraped areas will appear lighter, the impression will be one of softly modeled forms.

K3 A Plaster Relief from a Plasticine Mould

Plasticine (also glitter-wax, potter's clay, etc.), strip of cardboard, plaster of Paris, mixing bowl, spoon, etc.

The design, using a knife, pencil, spatula, etc., is worked in intaglio into a rectangular or oval plasticine slab, which should be 1/2 to 1 inch thick. The subjects will again be comparatively large and uncomplicated figures ('Horse and Rider,' 'The Cyclist,' etc.). Tools and materials also make this technique particularly suitable for purely decorative themes. It is only necessary to recall the incredible feats performed by some cooks in the decoration of butter or sugar icing.

To hold the plaster in position, stick a cardboard strip into the plasticine along the edges. Then the plaster, mixed with an equal quantity of water, is poured in. An almost infinite number of casts can be taken from this type of mould (*Plate 16c*).

K4 Plaster Casts from Lino Cuts

Lino cut (see H5), wooden battens, plaster of Paris, mixing bowl, spoon, etc., for mixing.

There are many ways of using lino cuts, apart from taking prints or rubbings (see H5, H6, H7, H8, H9). The student can also make casts, *i.e.* reliefs.

The lino cut, picture up, is placed on a table and surrounded by an improvised batten frame. This is all that is needed by way of a mould. The linoleum does not require treatment with wax, soap, etc. Then make the plaster mixture, using water and plaster in equal proportions, and pour it into the frame. To avoid bubbles, tap against the table from time to time. When the plaster has set, from ten to twenty minutes, the lino cut can be detached without any difficulty.

There are several ways of treating the cast. A lino cut made for a drawing with white outlines (see H5) will produce raised lines, one made for white figures on a black ground, a full relief, etc. To make the raised portions more distinct, coat the whole slab with a thin layer of color and then go over it with a damp rag or sandpaper. This will confine the color to the ground, thus making the figures appear lighter (*Plate 17a*).

Plaster Intaglio

K 5

Plaster slab (see K 1), pen-knife (or lino cutting tools).

The design, first outlined in pencil, is carved and scraped out of the plaster slab in intaglio, *i.e.* the forms, instead of being raised, are hollowed out. Again, three-dimensional effects must be avoided. This technique has several possible uses.

a. Baking Moulds

Baking moulds are normally made of wood, though a plaster mould, provided it is coated with a layer of olive oil or some other edible oil, will do equally well.

b. Wax and Clay Reliefs

Glitter-wax or potter's clay is carefully pressed into the mould in small pieces. The mould needs no special preparation, except that the plaster must be kept dry in the case of wax and wet for clay. The casts are easily detached. It is also possible to cast in hot melted wax, in which case the mould will have to be equipped with an improvised frame (lid of a cardboard box, etc.).

c. Papier-mâché Reliefs

The mould is lined with small pieces of damp tissue paper. Then it is filled with successive layers of strips of paper—newspaper, etc.—soaked in wallpaper paste (up to ten layers). The cast can be removed only when it has dried completely. The top layer, *i.e.*, the layer first inserted in the mould, can then be painted, varnished, coated with paste, etc.

d. Plaster Reliefs

In the case of taking plaster casts, the mould has to be especially prepared. The simplest method consists in applying a coating of soap with a brush, wet rag, etc. All traces of foam must be carefully wiped off to avoid the formation of air bubbles. A well-fitting frame of wooden battens or cardboard is then formed round the mould, and the plaster mixture (water and plaster in equal proportions) is poured in. When the plaster has set, which will take between ten and twenty minutes, the cast can be easily detached. If there should be any difficulty, wait until the plaster is completely dry, when the two plaster slabs can be separated with gentle taps along the join, which has first been freed of any plaster that may have run over it in the course of pouring.

K6 Making a Plaster Cylinder

Plaster of Paris, clay or glitter-wax, jam jar, mixing bowl, pen-knife.

Baked clay cylinders carved in intaglio, for making reliefs in damp clay, were known to the ancient Babylonians. First make a plaster mixture (see E4), which is poured into an empty jam jar. When the plaster has hardened the glass is cracked with a hammer—it might be advisable to wrap the glass in an old newspaper to avoid injury from splinters—and removed. The remaining plaster cylinder, or roller, is then carved with the design. Only subjects involving figures are really suited to this technique. The relief is obtained by passing the cylinder

a Cardboard Engraving (H 13, relief), 'Swings,' by an eleven-year-old boy. Length 6½ inches

b Thread Print (H 15), 'Abstract Design,' by a sixteen-year-old boy. Length 20 inches

c Celluloid Engraving (H 14, intaglio), 'Town on a River,' by a student teacher. Width 9 inches

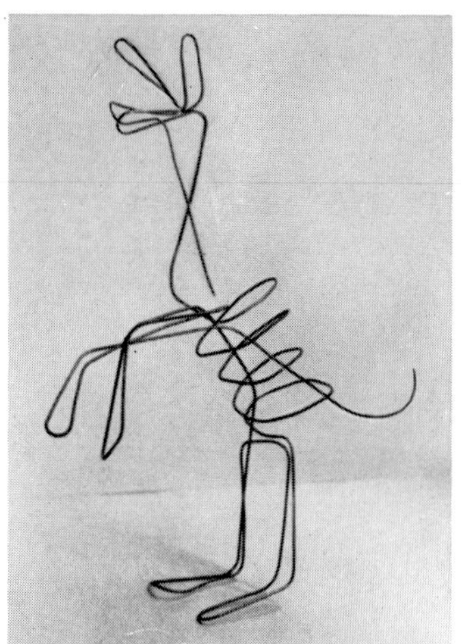

a Wire Sculpture (J3), 'Animal,' by a student teacher. Height 9¼ inches

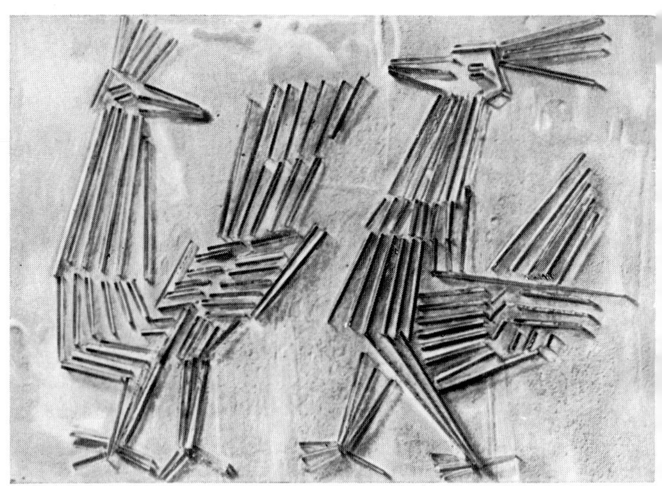

b Glass Fragments Set in Cement (F7 and F9), 'Birds in Conversation,' by a student teacher. Length 26 inches

c Masks from Paper Bags (J9), 'Ghosts,' by student teachers

a Modeling in Plasticine (J 6), 'Man in a Boat,' by an eight-year-old boy. Length 4 inches

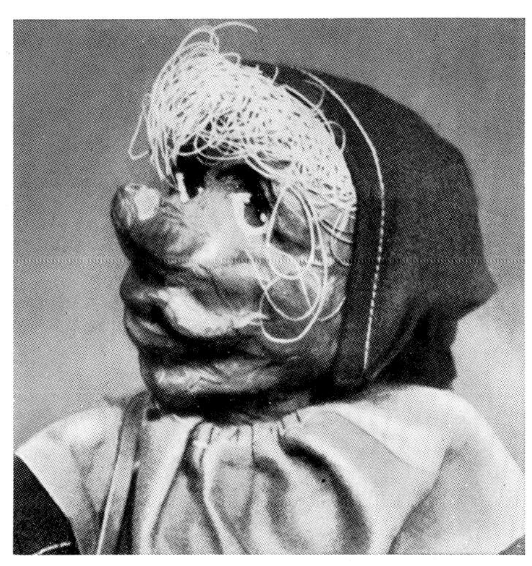

b Papier-Mâché Head (J 10)

c Plaster Casts from Plasticine Negatives (K 3), by adults students. Height about 6 inches

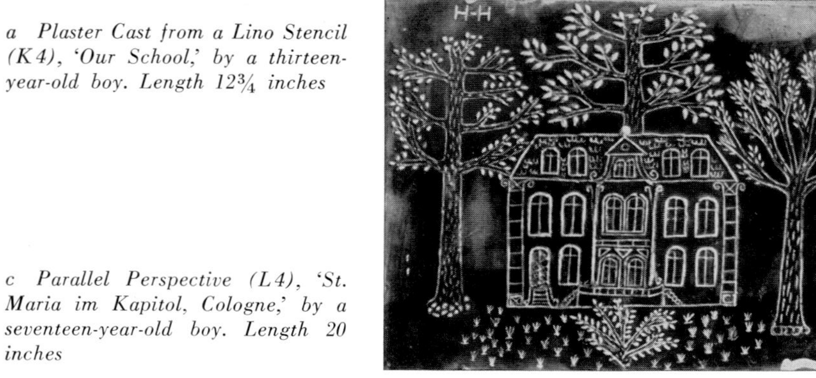

a Plaster Cast from a Lino Stencil (K4), 'Our School,' by a thirteen-year-old boy. Length 12¾ inches

c Parallel Perspective (L4), 'St. Maria im Kapitol, Cologne,' by a seventeen-year-old boy. Length 20 inches

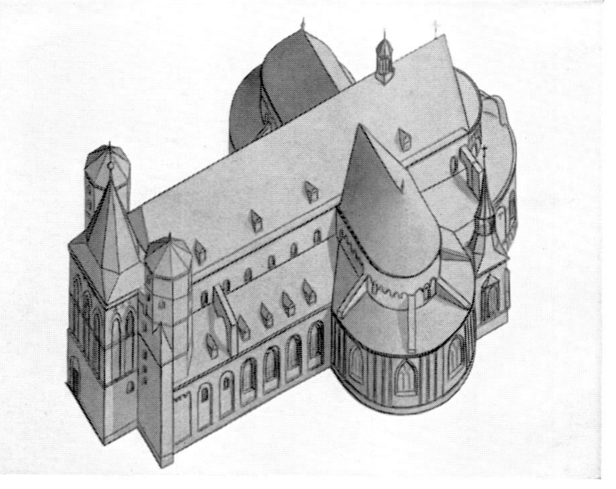

b Paper Relief (K7), 'Fantastic Bird,' by a student teacher. Height 20½ inches

a 'A Building in Progress' (L5), by a thirteen-year-old boy. Length 12¾ inches

b Architectural Fantasy in Glass (L8), by a student teacher. Height 8 inches

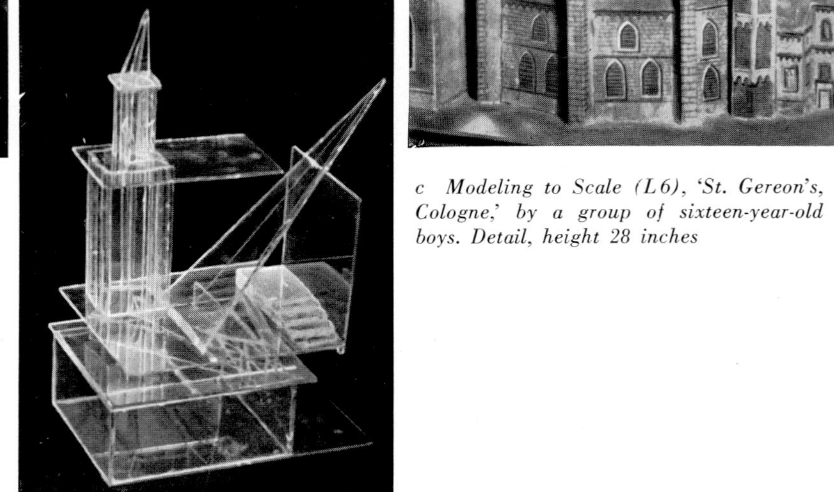

c Modeling to Scale (L6), 'St. Gereon's, Cologne,' by a group of sixteen-year-old boys. Detail, height 28 inches

a Cloth Batik (M1 and M2), 'Red Indian,' after a design by a thirteen-year-old boy. Length 40 inches

b Painting in Gold and Silver Leaf (M3 and O3), 'Musicians,' by a group of children, after a design by an eleven-year-old boy. Height 68 inches

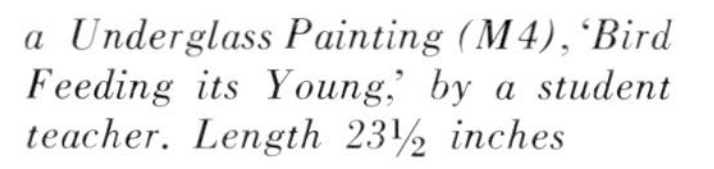

a *Underglass Painting (M4), 'Bird Feeding its Young,' by a student teacher. Length 23½ inches*

b *Large Jumping Jack in Cardboard (N2), by an eleven-year-old boy*

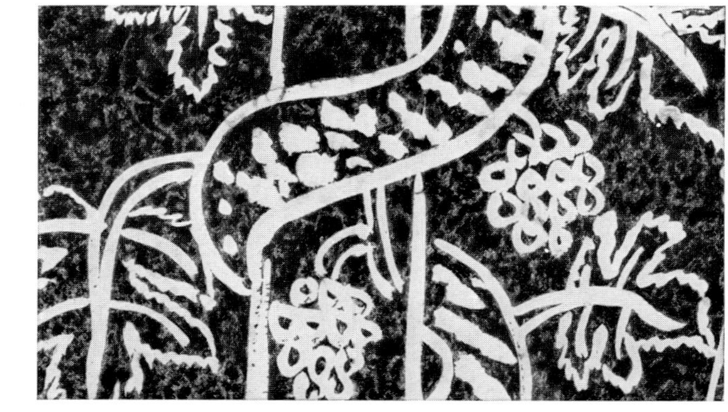

c *White Resist Painting (M4), 'Grape Harvest,' by a twelve-year-old boy. Detail, actual size*

a Direct Painting (B3a and O1), 'Skipping,' by a group of three six-year-old girls. Length 40 inches

b Joining Separate Contributions (O6), 'Wall Hanging for a Classroom.' Length 88 inches

Shadow-play Figure (D5). The movement is worked by the strings while the horse is held by the bars on the body. Length 11¼ inches

Plate 23

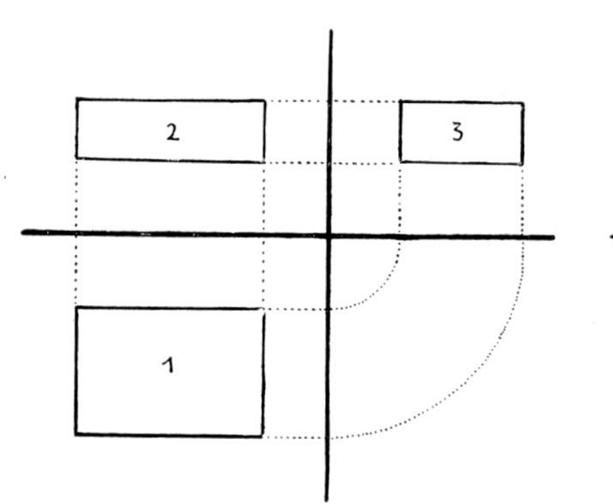

(1) Plan view
(2) Side elevation
(3) Front elevation

Three views and parallel projection of a church

a Projective Drawing (L3)

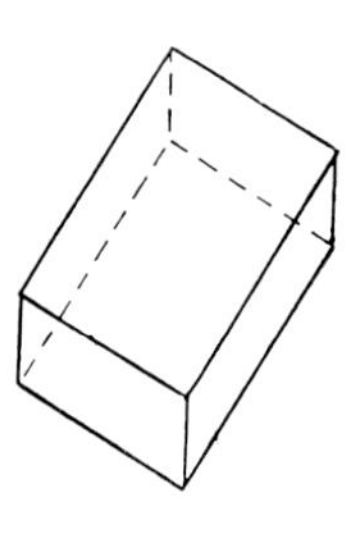

A brick

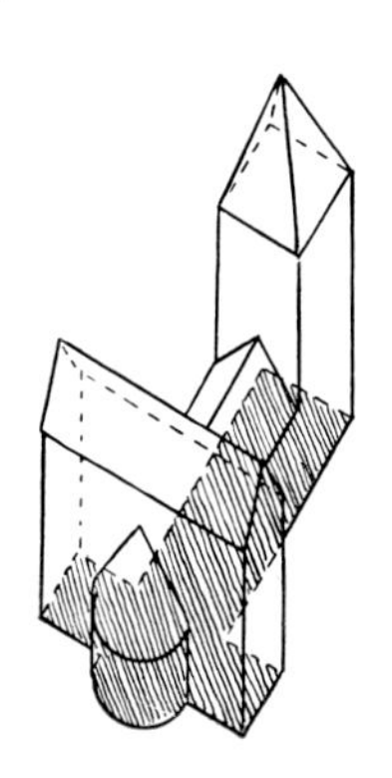

A church

b Isometric Drawing (L4)

over a clay slab about $^1/_2$ inch thick (*Plate 27b*). The plaster cylinder can also be used as a baking mould (see K5a).

Paper Relief

K7

Fairly stiff paper of any kind, scissors or razor blade.

Here, the aim is to exploit all the three-dimensional possibilities of paper folding, bending, rolling, etc. There are two basic techniques: cutting in one piece and cutting in several pieces.

a. Cutting in One Piece

Design a fairly large silhouette-like figure—a bird or fish, etc.—which is treated in the manner described under D1, except that the result is obtained by merely cutting into the paper and folding or rolling back, rather than by cutting out scales, feathers, or markings, etc. The possibilities of the material will become revealed in the rhythmic repetition of similar elements rather than in the search for variety for its own sake (*Plate 17b*).

b. Cutting in Several Pieces

One can also add forms cut or folded in paper instead of cutting into the 'ground.' In this case—unless all the work is done by folding and inserting through slits or plaiting—some adhesive will also be necessary.

Tin Relief

K8

Thin sheet metal, including old tin cans, metal scissors (possibly also pliers, hammer, nails, wire), piece of strong cardboard or plywood.

This technique is best suited to objects and figures of clear and simple construction. The separate portions are cut out, rolled or cut into, and attached to the plywood or paper ground. Methods of joining have to be discovered by experience. Wire loops, a kind of sewing with thin wire, and bolt-like wire clips have all been found satisfactory. Altogether, this technique leaves plenty of scope for inventiveness (*Plate 25a*).

K 9 Foil Relief

Aluminium or copper foil, hardwood modeling tools, newspaper or felt to protect the table or work bench.

These sheets of foil (cooking foil, etc.) are worked from the back. To make an impression, the base must be resilient but firm, e.g., thick felt or several layers of newspaper, etc. Sculptor's tools, pieces of wood, or even a blunt pencil can be used. The finished work can be given a coat of color, the raised portions being afterwards polished blank with a soft rag.

K 10 Paper Relief on Clay

Newspaper, wallpaper paste, clay or plasticine, plywood base or table top, poster colors.

Using a suitable base, make a mask or even an entire relief in clay or plasticine, keeping to fairly large forms. Then build up ten layers of paper, the first merely soaked in water, the others in wallpaper paste, smoothing each carefully over the relief. The paper should be applied in pieces about 4 inches in diameter. After drying, the paper relief will lift off without any difficulty (*Plate 28b*). Only opaque colors can be used for painting, since the print would otherwise show.

L ARCHITECTURAL DRAWING AND MODELING

I DRAWING AND DESIGN

Free Designing

L1

Any kind of drawing paper, pencil, pen, charcoal, etc., possibly drawing-board, compasses, and ruler.

The subject determines the technique. Just as there is free painting and free drawing, there is also a way of designing without any preconceived ideas, following entirely a sense of proportion and a feeling for the statics and dynamics of architectural forms. It is this feeling, and not the technical knowledge of the structural engineer, out of which children should make their first efforts at architecture. A beginning might be made with a spontaneous design for a cottage, an exhibition pavilion, or even a whole town. Ruler and compasses should be dispensed with in this type of work, for which nothing beyond charcoal, pencil, or pen, and the cheapest type of paper are needed. More specific designs, for pieces to be used, such as bookshelves, etc., demand the translation of the original sketch into a fairly detailed drawing, for which a set square might be allowed if ruler and compasses should really prove inadequate. The type of drawing, whether isometry, free perspective, or a geometric perspective, will depend on the intention meant to be conveyed.

Measured Drawings

L2

Ruler, protractor (possibly drawing-board and T-square), pencil (medium hard, see A1), pen (possibly drawing pen), drawing ink, cartridge paper.

Suitable subjects include the façade of almost any building, a piece of furniture, garden fence and gate, etc., all seen at an angle of 90 degrees.

Measurements are either given or, better still taken by the pupil from the object in question. If this presents difficulties in the case of a larger building, the children can be allowed to estimate, since this is not primarily a question of mathematical accuracy. The scale will be about 1 in.:1 ft. to 2 in.:1 ft. for furniture, and between 1/16 in.:1 ft. and 1/8 in.:1 ft. for buildings. Distances can be judged in steps instead of using a tape-measure.

Normally, the pupils will begin their drawing with the base. The principal outlines come first, then doors, windows, etc., and finally decorative detail.

L 3 Projective Drawing

Materials as above.

By projective drawing is meant the vertical projections of a body to three planes. One distinguishes between plan view, side elevation, and front elevation. This technique can be demonstrated very simply with a brick, lit up by a flashlight against the corner of a room. There will be three possible shadow projections:

(1) to the ground, the stone slightly raised and lit from above—plan view;
(2) lit frontally—front elevation; and
(3) lit sideways—side elevation.

How all these views are fitted into one drawing is shown in *Plate 23a*. Exactly the same rules apply to the representation of more complicated objects. A beginning can be made with pieces of furniture, a well-known building, etc.

Occasionally, there might be some detail not visible from a certain angle, though of considerable structural importance. This can be drawn in by dotted lines (a house partly hidden by a garden wall, etc.).

Parallel Perspective (Isometric Drawing)

Materials as above.

This technique presupposes an acquaintance with projective drawing (see L3). Start again with the three principal views. The ground plan—and this is important—appears in its original shape, but turned by an angle of, say, 30 or 60 degrees. The building is then 'raised' by transferring the measurements from the two other views to the plan view, which thus assumes a third dimension (*Plate 23b*). Where necessary, *i.e.*, where invisible in real life, the different points are connected with dotted lines.

Isometric drawing is the most common type of perspective. It is not, strictly speaking, accurate, since there would normally be some foreshortening, unless the building is seen directly from above, and not turned at an angle as in our drawing. Yet our natural sense of perspective is not disturbed by such apparent incongruities. Experience has shown that isometric perspective is merely a development of the child's intuitive rendering of the third dimension, in contrast to parallel perspective, which is utterly alien to children and should therefore have no place in the curriculum until much later, if at all.

In the case of more complicated forms—a Romanesque church with towers, etc. (*Plate 17c*)—construct each portion (nave, transepts, choir, towers) separately above the plan, removing lines not meant to show afterwards.

II ARCHITECTURAL MODELING

L5 A Building in Progress

Cardboard or paper, small wooden stakes and battens, thread, adhesive, poster colors, scissors and pen-knife.

Though the children can be given some simple directions, they ought to find their own individual solutions (*Plate 18a*). If instructions are given too early, the child will often remain completely unaware of the problems involved in the handling of a particular material. It is therefore better to arouse interest in the task rather than to emphasize the technical aspect. With the awakening of the imagination, the ability to cope with technical problems will also grow.

L6 Modeling to Scale

Thin cardboard, etc., gummed paper, glue or similar adhesive (e. g., cold glue, etc.), paste, poster colors, scissors, pen-knife, bristle brush.

A building modeled to scale is an achievement of which children, and even adults, can feel justly proud.

Begin with a design of your own or a measured drawing (see L2). In the case of historical buildings guess the proportions from photographs or by rough measurements (counting steps, etc.). The first drawings (plan view, side elevation, front elevation, see L3) should be as accurate as possible, keeping to a scale no smaller than 1:100. Then the ground plan is transferred to a cardboard or plywood base, on which the model is raised. It is usually easier to make the parts separately and to assemble them afterwards, rather than to attempt the whole building in one piece. Each piece is drawn on the piece of cardboard out of which it is to be cut, taking care to make it in as few sections as possible. After cutting out, the edges are creased with a knife or paper folder so that they will form clean corners. More complicated forms—towers, etc.—can be made separately. Finally, all the sections are carefully joined with glue (along the sides) and gummed tape (for strengthening the corners). The whole building is then given several coats of paste-bound poster color, mixed to a fairly thick consistency. This will also hold the model together. To prevent warping, there should be no attempt at quick drying. Internal supports in the form of diagonally placed sticks will also help. The final detail can be drawn in with the brush. Small modeled additions, such as cornices, porticos, etc., will enhance the work considerably (*Plate 18c*).

Building in Paper

L 7

Cartridge paper, etc., adhesive (cold glue, milk-glue, etc.), scissors or razor blade.

The characteristics of the material can be brought out to the full in paper building, particularly in designs for the paper stage. Any elaborate construction will be avoided; emphasis should be placed on folding out, cutting into, inserting, etc., rather than cutting out and pasting together. Trees, shrubs, any kind of fantastic architecture, and abstract forms are ideally suited to this white-on-white technique.

Architectural Fantasy in Glass (wire, battens, corrugated paper, etc.)

L 8

Glass fragments, glass cutter, ruler, all-purpose adhesive.

Glass, provided the edges are cut absolutely straight to make a clean join, can, like cardboard or plywood, be used for architectural models. There is no warping, and the original form is retained under all conditions. The material has a considerable beauty, even magic, of its own. Glass models should therefore not be copies of actual buildings, but products of the child's imagination (*Plate 18b*). Similarly, a vast range of other materials (sticks, battens, corrugated paper, etc.) can be used in the creation of fantastic structures.

M APPLIED DECORATION

I PAINTING

M1 Batik

a. Paper Batik

Thin fairly absorbent paper (sugar paper, etc.), newspapers as a working base, bits of old candles, wood stain in glowing colors (red, green, etc.), used tins for mixing the colors, double saucepan, gas ring or hot plate, etc., flat iron, bristle brush, brush for applying the wax.

First sketch the design—which should be strictly two-dimensional, since anything else would be contrary to the character of this technique—on the batik paper, using a soft pencil or charcoal. Then, place the sheet on a carefully smoothed layer of newspaper (one or two sheets). The candle remains have meanwhile been heated almost to boiling point in a double saucepan. Care must be taken not to bring the wax to actual boiling point, since it is highly inflammable. An electric ring is always preferable to an open flame, a double saucepan to direct heating. The wax is applied with the brush along the outlines, or over whole areas, depending on the type of picture intended (*Plate 24a*). No color will adhere to the waxed portions. If several colors are used, always begin with the lightest, working gradually towards the darkest. Each colored section is covered in wax (there is no need, in the case of paper batik, to wait until the color has dried before applying the wax). Wood stain for cheapness is suggested, but there are a number of cheap and excellent batik dyes on the market, and these may well be found more convenient for class work.

After finishing with the colors, a sheet of newspaper is placed over the work and carefully ironed to remove the wax. As a result of ironing, the paper will become 'oiled' and trans-

a Paper Batik (M 1a), 'Animal with FruitBowl', by a fourteen-year-old boy. Length 22$^1/_2$ inches

b Direct Painting with Poster Colors (B 3a), 'Ploughing', by a thirteen-year-old boy. Length 18$^1/_2$ inches

parent, thereby greatly increasing the brilliance of the colors. If the newspapers used for the base should stick, they can be easily detached by warming one of the corners with the iron.

b. Cloth Batik

Thin silk or cotton with an absolutely smooth surface (no rep, etc.), old newspapers as a working base, cold fabric dyes, double saucepan for warming the wax, electric ring, iron, bristle brush (or a special container for pouring the wax), separate bowl for each color.

Fabric batik differs very little from paper batik in technique, except in a few, though important, points. The wax must penetrate the fabric completely (if necessary it must be applied on both sides). Instead of having the colors applied with the brush, the material has to be left to soak in the cold dyes, preferably without creasing. It must also be allowed to dry completely before each new layer of wax. Before being given the final, and darkest, coat of dye, the fabric is thoroughly creased to obtain the characteristic batik effect, which is the result of the color penetrating through the small cracks in the waxed surface. The wax is ironed out on old newspapers, the last remains being removed by soaking in warm water (*Plate 19a*).

Note: In painting with wax, either work on a base of old newspapers—which means that the work must be detached from its base each time before applying the color—or use a frame, possibly stretching the material over a large basin, etc. In either case, the fabric will have to be firmly stretched, and if necessary tacked to the base with drawing pins. New fabrics are unsuitable for batik, unless they have first been washed.

Fabric Painting

M2

Smooth or textured fabrics (texture can play an important part in fabric painting; experiments in different materials are therefore highly recommended), special fabric dyes, hair or bristle brush (depending on the type of fabric, choice of subject, etc.), palette (or a shallow plate as a substitute), old newspapers or embroidery frame, drawing pins.

Any suggestion of perspective would be completely out of place (*Plate 19a*). The technique differs little from any other form of painting. The fabric has to be stretched, either on a table over a newspaper base or in a frame. Only special branded fabric dyes are fast. Where fastness is no consideration, almost any other kind of color (drawing ink, wood stain, poster colors, etc.) can be used.

M3 Painting in Gold and Silver Leaf

Paper of any kind (from old newspapers to brown paper and wallpaper remains), a slow-drying oil varnish, gold or silver leaf, poster colors, bristle brush, soft brush.

First draw a design—perhaps provisionally in pencil or charcoal—in poster colors. A suitable subject might be a fish, whose body is covered in fairly large scales. Head, fins, and tail could be painted gold, the scales silver. Then the oil varnish is carefully applied to the outlined areas. Work of this kind demands a little skill, which comes with experience. Any surplus gold or silver leaf is carefully removed with the brush. The colored outlines should be left standing; the background might even be filled in with black or some other dark color. The general effect should be that of a jewel glittering against the dark (*Plate 19b*).

Variation: Bronze powder can take the place of gold or silver leaf. A bronze painting or bronze brush drawing has a beauty of its own. It is also possible to use bronze and gold and silver leaf in the same picture (*Plate 33*).

Drying is slow, particularly in the case of gold and silver leaf, and the work, until it has completely set, will therefore be highly sensitive to touch, even to gentle pressure.

Underglass Painting

M4

Pane of glass, poster colors, soft brush (possibly a special poster color brush).

Painting with poster colors under glass, a technique highly suited to children, presents few difficulties if certain rules are observed.

1. The easiest way is to make a colored brush drawing, using a soft brush. The colors, in this case, can almost cover the glass. What little remains of the ground (between blades of grass in a meadow or the feathers of a bird, etc.) can be backed with paper of a contrasting color (black, etc.) (*Plate 20a*).

2. None of the glass might be left to show. Care must be taken not to smudge the colors which have already dried. Wet painting, unless certain effects are aimed at, must be avoided.

3. In the most advanced form of underglass painting—the kind found in peasant art—the brush drawing is backed by several layers of painting. To avoid smudging, each layer must be applied very quickly so that the colors below—which are seen as the top layer from above in the final picture—have no time to dissolve and blur, or be protected with a coat of varnish.

White Resist Painting

M5

White gouache or tempera color, black ink or poster color, pen or brush, cartridge paper.

First make a white pen or brush drawing, in gouache or tempera color, on the white paper. When the drawing has dried, the entire sheet is covered in black drawing ink or poster color (*Plate 20c*). As the ink dries, it disperses over the white paint. The drying process can be slowed down by dampening.

M6 Color Resist Painting

Cartridge paper, etc., gouache colors, brush, drawing ink.

White resist painting has already been discussed (see M5). If colors are used in place of white, the ink will again disperse over the areas of paint—provided only branded gouache or designer's colors are used. The colors will be almost unaffected by dampening.

M7 Painting Small Boxes (match boxes, etc.)

Match box, etc., poster colors, wax (beeswax, furniture polish, etc.), or size.

The student must always ask himself whether decoration is justified. Any applied design must emphasize rather than deny function. A simple box is not meant to display landscapes or tell stories. Any appropriate design will merely stress shape and outline.

M8 Easter Eggs

(a) Direct painting: poster colors, soft brush.

(b) Wax drawing: wax, double saucepan, small stick for applying the wax.

For (a) see Painting with Poster Colors, B3; for (b) see Batik, M1a, except that a small sharpened stick will be found more suitable for applying the wax. After the egg has been decorated with wax and immersed in the cold dye, it is rubbed dry with a warm cloth.

In painting any object, the student must consider its shape, in the case of an egg no less than in a chair or wardrobe. Any landscapes, or scenes from fairy tales, etc., would therefore be quite unsuitable. Stars at the tips and stripes to follow the curved surface are far more appropriate. Possibilities are almost unlimited. Here, as always, the emphasis should be on rhythmic repetition rather than a profusion of forms.

Painting with Oil Crayons (A 2 and B 2), 'Our Family', by a six-year-old girl. Height 24$^3/_4$ inches

II OTHER DECORATIVE TECHNIQUES

Paste Paper

M9

A fairly non-absorbent paper, wallpaper paste, powder colors or poster colors, drawing ink, etc., flat brush, cardboard, scissors.

A sheet of fairly non-absorbent paper, resting on several layers of newspaper which have been placed on the table as a working base, is given a first coat of paste, and, when this has been completely absorbed, a second. Then apply the color, either in liquid form, or as a powder mixed with very little water, and distribute it with the fingers or the simplest tools (bits of cardboard, comb, etc.). All kinds of effects can be produced, and the work can be corrected again and again while the paste is still wet. Paste colors, instead of 'running,' form ridges. The resulting texture is one of their great attractions.

This technique is as suitable for making pictures as for purely decorative purposes.

Pin Drawing

M10

Darning needle and paper (any kind).

This technique is a well-known form of popular art, where it is invariably used for purely decorative work. It would be quite unsuitable for making pictures. In decorating a cardboard box, etc., it is best to make a preliminary pencil drawing, preferably some strictly two-dimensional design, which is then pierced with many small pin-pricks. These must not be placed too closely, since the characteristic effect is achieved by the contrast between pierced and plain areas rather than pierced outlines alone.

Matchstick Pictures

M11

Matches or other small sticks, drawing pad, etc., adhesive.

Before gluing the matches into their final position, experiment freely until the desired form is obtained. Several rules can be set. All the matches might have to be run horizontally, vertically, at certain angles, etc. (*Plate 29a*). Figures should be built up rather than outlined (see *Plate 15b*; text under F7 and F9d.).

M12 Cardboard Sgraffito

Colored cardboard, scissors, or razor blade.

Sgraffito is not really the right name for this technique (see E10). Only the arrangement of several layers of differently colored material (cardboard instead of sand or cement) justifies the use of the term. By cutting into a layer of cardboard, the color of the layer below will be revealed, exactly as when working in sand sgraffito (E10).

M13 Colored Cement Inlay

Cement, powder colors, mixing bowls, sand.

Cement and sand, in the proportion of one part of cement to two parts of sand, are mixed with water to a thick consistency. Some of this mixture is dyed with liquid powder colors, though care must be taken not to dilute too much, if the setting process is not to be unduly prolonged or even endangered. The colored cement is then arranged on a suitable base (pane of glass, plywood, lino, etc.) like a picture. There should be distinct areas of color rather than intricate designs. Then the plain cement mixture is applied to the thickness required to form a slab. After two days, when the cement has set, the whole slab can be lifted off. Cement, unlike plaster, takes a long time to set, but does not adhere to the base, which therefore will not need any preparation by oiling, etc.

M14 Stucco Inlay

Plaster of Paris, powder colors, mixing bowls, wooden battens, pen-knife, piece of pumice.

a Folding Cut (D3), 'Faces'

b Soft Toys (N1), by student teachers

c Slag Block Carving (J7), 'Pig,' by a student teacher

a Slate Relief (K2), 'Cat,' by a student teacher

b Clay Relief, made with a plaster cylinder (K6), 'Elephant Train,' by a seventeen-year-old girl. $11\frac{1}{4} \times 4\frac{1}{2}$ inches

a Tin Relief (K8), 'Red Indian with Spear,' by a group of children, after the design of a seven-year-old boy. Height 32 inches

b Paper Relief on Plasticine (K 10), 'St. Michael,' by a group of children, after a design by a fourteen-year-old boy

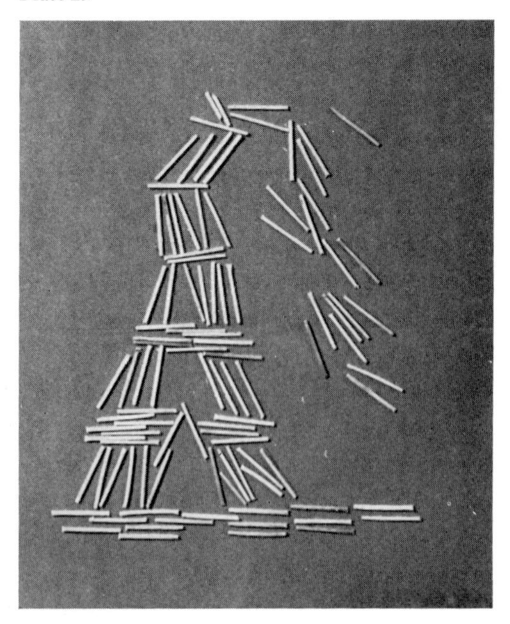

a Matchstick Picture (M 11), 'Falling Tower,' by a student teacher. Height 20 inches

b Wire Picture (M 17), 'Red Indian,' by a group of children, after a design by a seven-year-old boy

First make a plaster slab (see E4) on which the design is outlined in pencil and then retraced with a sharp instrument. The areas to be inlaid are then scraped off with a knife to a depth of no more than 1/4 inch and filled with a fairly liquid mixture of colored plaster (for making colored plaster see F8). Each area of color has to be separately filled in, left to dry, and polished with a piece of pumice stone under the running tap to make it level with the surface. The finished picture can be given a coat of liquid wax or size.

Cement or Stucco Bowls and Vases over a Clay or Plasticine Core

M15

Cement or plaster of Paris, clay or plasticine, mixing bowl, sand (for cement only).

The form of a bowl or vase is modeled in solid clay or plasticine . A not-too-liquid cement (using sand and cement in equal proportions or one part of cement to two parts of sand) or plaster mixture (see E4) is then applied over this core to a thickness of between 1/2 and 1 inch, depending on the size of the vase or bowl. After drying (in the case of cement two days, plaster 15 minutes), the core can be removed. Possible forms of decoration are cement inlay (see M13), and even a plaster picture (see E4) or stucco or cement mosaic, in which case small mosaic pieces have to be stuck to the surface of the core (with gum, etc.) before the plaster or cement mixture is applied.

Newspaper and Poster Collage

M16

Pieces of poster or newspaper, also other paper with an interesting surface texture (corrugated paper, etc.), adhesive, scissors.

All the pieces of cut-out paper are carefully arranged on a sheet of newspaper or cartridge paper, etc., until they form a balanced composition. Headlines, large capitals, single figures cut from photographs, etc., and even geometric forms cut from newspapers or almost any other kind of textured paper, are particularly effective. Any riot of form should be avoided in this technique, where success is largely a matter of careful balance and originality.

M17 Wire Pictures

All kinds of wire, pliers.

Wire pictures can either be treated as mobiles, stretched in a frame to be hung on the wall like a drawing (*Plate 34*), or stretched across nails on a board, etc. Although the outlines should be very distinct, the picture ought not to consist of outline only. Interesting effects can be obtained within each area by using different kinds of wire (*Plate 29b*), forming intricate, almost filigree-like patterns. Even wire of another color (brass, copper, etc.) can be introduced. The ends are looped or suitably tied to keep the composition in place.

N TOYS

Soft Toys

N1

Bits of fabric, needle and thread, paper for drawing.

The basic form of a soft toy is extremely simple (*Plate 26b*). It resembles a sack, made up of two identical parts, which are sewn together and filled with bits of rag, cotton wool, etc. Having drawn a pattern, which should be as uncomplicated as possible, it can be cut out. When sewing up, a hole must be left to insert the stuffing. More elaborate figures may require gussets, etc. Ears and eyes can be sewn on afterwards.

Jumping Jack

N2

Plywood or strong cardboard, fretsaw, wood drill, sandpaper, poster colors (possibly clear varnish), thread, thin wire.

Head, body, arms, and legs (possibly in two parts, to be later joined at the knees) are cut out separately. The parts are then joined with thin wire through small holes made with the wood drill. The wire is carefully twisted on each side, allowing at the same time for movement. All the operating threads are orientated towards a central axis.

As in all children's work, everything will depend on the use of the imagination, on bright colors, and original forms (*Plate 20b*). A final coat of size or colorless varnish will protect against dirt and fading.

Branchwood Carvings

N3

Fresh twigs, a sharp pen-knife, handsaw, push brace.

Stick carving, like the carving of toys or chessmen, is a time-honored technique. The bark is removed in places and the white wood exposed and cut into, though only where this is absolutely necessary. To make a toy with fixed or movable limbs, holes will have to be drilled. Branchwood animals with fitted necks, heads, horns, and tails can be most attractive.

N4 Large Animal Masks

Brown paper, strip of cardboard, old newspapers, fabric remains, wooden battens, etc., wallpaper paste, scissors, saw, bristle brush, strip of gummed paper.

Masks, having to be placed over the head, must be both light and of firm construction. First make a frame, either of cardboard strips or, in the case of large masks (a crocodile, etc.), of wooden battens. The cardboard or paper strips are held together with strips of gummed tape to form oval rings, which are loosely intersected until the basic form of the head is achieved. Eyes, ears, etc., can be added at this stage or later. The 'skull' is then covered with layers of paper which have first been soaked in paste. Work will be very much easier if each layer is allowed to dry before the next is applied. Three to four layers are generally sufficient. An opening must be left so that the mask can be put on. The finished mask is painted in powder colors, bound with paste or glue. Details like fiery nostrils or staring eyes can then be worked out. A lion might be given a mane from wood shavings, a bull wooden horns, etc.

Wax Engraving (E 1), 'Funeral' by an eight-year-old girl. Length 22 inches

O COMMUNAL WORK

All the techniques described in these pages are also suitable for groups of pupils. What could be a better decoration for the classroom than some work carried out by the whole class? Quite often, the total of contributions will reach a standard that would have been beyond the abilities of most individual pupils.

I ORGANIZATION

Communal work can be organized along different lines:

Joint Activities O1

According to the size of the work (an entire wall, etc.) a limited number of children can take part at the same time (*Plate 1*). If the whole class is to be included each child or group of children can take its turn (*Plate 21a*). Both solutions are possible, depending on the nature of the task (*Plate 34*).

Joining Separate Contributions O2

An entirely different situation arises when each child works on its own, the individual contributions being joined later (*Plate 8a*). This requires a certain amount of planning in regard to scale, etc. (*Plate 5a*). Designs might include figures and trees for a theme like 'Runners in the Forest.' Both figures and trees are to be silhouttes, to be joined in a large communal picture. Special attention will therefore have to be given to proportion.

O3 Joint Execution of an Individual Design

All the children might submit designs for a large tapestry, etc. The winning design is worked by the whole class (*Plates 9a, 19b, 28a, 28b and 29b*).

O4 Splitting up and Reassembling a Design

Sometimes the design—for a large picture, etc.—can be split up according to the number of pupils. Since each child will work separately, special attention has to be given to joins in color, material, etc. (*Plate 2*).

O5 Distribution of Tasks

In many cases, the work can be broken up into different processes. In the case of mosaic, some children might be making the plaster mixture, while others prepare the colors (see Plaster Mosaic, F8) (*Plate 32*).

O6 Joining Separate Works

Occasionally, completely independent works can be joined. This applies to such projects as embroideries, cut-outs, series of pictures (*Plate 21b*).

II TYPES OF COMMUNAL WORK

These will depend on the choice of technique, the particular needs of the class, and many other factors.

Individual contributions can be joined to a frieze or chequer board design, or to single pictures. The figures in a procession will suggest a frieze, square lino cuts of the same size and theme a chequer board, silhouttes of a subject like 'Runners in the Forest' a large picture.

Lino Print (H 5), 'Friends,' by a sixteen-year-old girl. Height 18 inches

Mosaic on a Sand-and-Paste Base (F6), 'Fantastic Bird,' by a group of twelve-year-old girls. Length 22 inches

Gold and silver leaf, bronze and tempera picture (M3), 'Tiger and Bird,' by two student teachers. 52 × 36 inches

Wire Picture on Wire Netting, set in a frame (M17), 'Gold and Silver Bird,' by a group of children and student teachers.
$39^{1}/_{2} \times 30$ *inches*

In the case of a large picture or wall hanging, the division into sections can be arbitrary or strictly geometric. Emphasis might be on the vertical-horizontal axis or the diagonal, or the division could appear more 'accidental.'

Obviously, several techniques do not admit of division. But even in large mosaic or fresco painting, a task can usually be found for each child.